DATA STRUCTURES IN PASCAL

A LABORATORY COURSE

DATA STRUCTURES IN PASCAL
A LABORATORY COURSE

JAMES ROBERGÉ
Illinois Institute of Technology

D. C. HEATH AND COMPANY

LEXINGTON, MASSACHUSETTS • TORONTO

Address editorial correspondence to:

D. C. Heath and Company
125 Spring Street
Lexington, MA 02173

Acquisitions Editor: Randall Adams
Developmental Editor: Karen H. Myer
Production Editor: Sarah Doyle
Designer: Jan Shapiro
Production Coordinator: Lisa Merrill

Published simultaneously in Canada.

Printed in the United States of America.

International Standard Book Number: 0–669–29523–X

10 9 8 7 6 5 4 3 2 1

*To my parents
for showing me what is possible,
and to my wife
for showing me why.*

To the Student

OBJECTIVES

The courses that I enjoyed most when I was a student were those that emphasized design. In design courses, I used the concepts taught in lecture to solve practical problems. The process of applying ideas made it easier for me to understand them and how they could be applied in a real-world setting.

This emphasis on learning by doing is used throughout *Data Structures in Pascal: A Laboratory Course.* In each laboratory, you explore a particular data structure by implementing it. As you create the implementation, you learn how the data structure works and how it can be applied. The resulting implementation is a working piece of software that you can use in later laboratories and programming projects.

ORGANIZATION OF THE LABORATORIES

Each laboratory consists of three parts: Prelab, In-lab, and Postlab. The **Prelab** exercise is a homework assignment in which you create an implementation of a data structure using the techniques that your instructor presents in lecture, along with material from your textbook. The **In-lab** phase consists of four exercises. In the first exercise, you test and debug the software that you developed in the Prelab. The remaining exercises apply or extend the concepts introduced in the Prelab. The last phase of each laboratory, the **Postlab,** is a homework assignment in which you analyze a data structure in terms of its efficiency or use.

Your instructor will specify which exercises you need to complete for each laboratory. Use the cover sheet provided with the laboratory to keep track of the exercises you have been assigned.

STUDENT DISK

The Student Disk accompanying this manual contains a set of software tools that make it easier for you to develop software. Each laboratory includes a visualization procedure that displays a given data structure. You can use this procedure to watch how your routines change the contents and organization of the data structure. Each laboratory also includes an interactive test program that you can use to help you test and debug your software.

Additional files containing data, partial solution shells, and other supporting routines also are provided on the Student Disk. The README file lists the files used in each laboratory. As you read a laboratory exercise, look for the floppy disk icon in the left margin. This icon indicates that the text is referring to a file on the Student Disk. You will need to use this file in order to complete the exercise. The floppy disk icon next to this paragraph, for example, is signaling you to look at the README file.

To the Instructor

OBJECTIVES

Four years ago, I was given the opportunity to introduce laboratories into my data structures course. I jumped at the chance because I saw laboratories as a way of involving students as active, creative partners in the learning process. By making the laboratories the focal point of the course, I sought to immerse students in the course material. I wanted to challenge them and yet to provide the structure, feedback, and support that they needed to meet the challenge. This manual is the product of four years of experimentation in working toward this objective. The laboratories emphasize creativity in both programming and analysis.

ORGANIZATION OF THE LABORATORIES

When I first began using laboratories, I attempted to shoehorn the creative process into a series of two-hour laboratories. The result was a pressure cooker that challenged everyone, but helped no one. In experimenting with solutions to this problem, I developed a laboratory framework that retains the creative element but shifts the time-intensive aspects outside the laboratory period. Within this structure, each laboratory includes three parts: Prelab, In-lab, and Postlab.

PRELAB

The Prelab exercise is a homework assignment that bridges the gap between the lecture and the laboratory period. In the Prelab, students explore and create on their own and at their own pace. Their goal is to synthesize the information they learn in the lecture with the material from their textbook to produce a working piece of software, usually an implementation of an abstract data type (ADT). A Prelab assignment—including a review of the relevant lecture and textbook materials—typically takes an evening to complete (that is, four to five hours).

IN-LAB

The In-lab section takes place during the actual laboratory period (assuming that you are using a closed laboratory setting). Each In-lab consists of four exercises, and each exercise has a distinct role.

The first In-lab exercise asks students to test the software they developed in the Prelab. The students create (or modify) a test plan that they then use to evaluate their code. This assignment provides an opportunity for students to receive immediate feedback on their Prelab work and to resolve any difficulties they might have encountered. It should take students approximately one hour to finish this exercise.

In Exercise 2, students apply the software they developed in the Prelab to a real-world problem that has been honed to its essentials to fit comfortably within the closed laboratory environment. Exercise 2 takes approximately one and a half hours to complete.

The last two exercises stress programming and provide a capstone to the Prelab. Each exercise takes approximately one hour to complete.

Most students will not be able to complete all four In-lab assignments within a typical closed laboratory period. I have provided a range of exercises so that you can select those that best suit your laboratory environment and your students' needs.

POSTLAB

The last phase of each laboratory is a homework assignment that is done following the laboratory period. In the Postlab, students analyze the efficiency or utility of a given data structure. Each Postlab exercise should take roughly thirty minutes to complete.

USING THE THREE-PART ORGANIZATION IN YOUR LABORATORY ENVIRONMENT

The term laboratory is used by computer science instructors to denote a broad range of environments. One group of students in my data structures course, for example, attends a closed two-hour laboratory; at the same time, another group of students takes the class in a televised format and "attends" an open laboratory. In developing this manual, I therefore tried to create a laboratory format suitable for a variety of open and closed laboratory settings. How you use the three-part organization depends on your laboratory environment.

This manual has been tested in both open and closed laboratory environments. My colleagues and I have used the exercises for three years. The manual also was tested this past year at Vassar College.

TWO-HOUR CLOSED LABORATORY

PRELAB

I expect the students attending a two-hour closed laboratory to make a good-faith effort to complete the Prelab exercise before coming to the lab. Their work need not be perfect, but their effort must be real (roughly 80 percent correct).

IN-LAB

I use the first hour of the laboratory period to resolve any problems the students might have experienced in completing the Prelab. Exercise 1 provides a framework for testing and debugging the students' software. My intention is to give constructive feedback so that students leave the lab with working Prelab software—a significant accomplishment on their part.

During the second hour, I have students complete one of the remaining exercises to reinforce the concepts learned in the Prelab. You can choose the exercise by section or by student, or you can let the students decide which exercise to complete.

Students leave the lab having received feedback on their Prelab and In-lab work. You need not rigidly enforce the hourly divisions; a mix of activities keeps everyone interested and motivated.

POSTLAB

After the lab, the students complete one of the Postlab exercises and turn it in during the next laboratory period.

ONE-HOUR CLOSED LABORATORY

PRELAB

When I have only one hour for the closed laboratory, I ask students to complete both the Prelab exercise and In-lab Exercise 1 before coming to the lab. This work is turned in at the start of the period.

IN-LAB

During the laboratory period, the students complete one of the remaining In-lab exercises.

POSTLAB

Again, the students complete one of the Postlab exercises and submit it during the next laboratory period.

OPEN LABORATORY

In an open laboratory setting, I have the students complete the Prelab exercise, In-lab Exercise 1, one of the remaining In-lab exercises, and one of the Postlab exercises. You can stagger the submission of these exercises throughout the week or have students turn in the entire laboratory as a unit.

ADAPTING THE MANUAL TO YOUR COURSE

ORDER OF TOPICS

Each of us covers the course material in the order that we believe best suits our students' needs. To give instructors flexibility in the order of presentation, I have made the individual laboratories as independent of one another as possible. The following list describes the few remaining dependencies between laboratories.

- All laboratories assume an understanding of the use of .DEC (declaration or header) files and .PAS (operation) files in creating an implementation of an ADT. This topic is covered on pages 7–9.
- Laboratories 2 through 14 assume that students know how to use the interactive, command-driven test programs provided on the Student Disk accompanying the manual. This topic is discussed on pages 26 and 27.
- In order to complete Laboratory 7, students need the List ADT implementations that they create in Laboratories 2 and 3.
- Laboratory 8 requires the ListCreate, ListInsert, and ListShowStructure operations from Laboratory 3.

- The Stack ADT operations from Laboratory 4 are needed for In-Lab Exercise 2 in Laboratory 8.
- In-lab Exercise 2 in Laboratory 11 requires the List ADT operations from *one* of the following labs: 2, 3, or 6.
- The Token ADT operations from Laboratory 1 are needed for In-lab Exercise 2 in Laboratory 14.
- In-lab Exercise 4 in Laboratory 15 requires the Stack ADT operations from Laboratory 4.

I recommend starting with either Laboratory 1 or Laboratory 2 because they use an array-based implementation of an ADT. Your students are likely to be far more familiar with arrays than with linked lists; these laboratories offer them the chance to focus on the implementation and use of an ADT without the added complexities that linked lists introduce. You can cover the remaining laboratories in the order you deem best.

You might wonder why I placed the performance evaluation laboratory at the end of the manual (Laboratory 15). The reason is simple: everyone covers this topic at a different time. Rather than bury it in the middle of the manual, I put it at the end so that you can include it where it best serves your and your students' needs.

ADT IMPLEMENTATION

I designed the laboratories to complement a variety of approaches to implementing each ADT. All ADT definitions stress the use of data abstraction and generic data elements. As a result, you can adapt them with minimal effort to suit different implementation strategies.

For each ADT, a set of TYPE declarations that frame an implementation of the ADT is given as part of the corresponding Prelab exercise. I also use this TYPE declaration framework in the visualization routine that accompanies the laboratory. Should you elect to adopt a different implementation strategy, you need only specify alternative TYPE declarations and make minor modifications to the visualization routine. You do not need to change anything else in either the supplied software or the laboratory text itself.

DIFFERENCES BETWEEN THE MANUAL AND YOUR TEXT

I have found that minor variations in style between the approaches used in the textbook and the laboratory manual discourage students from simply copying material from the textbook. Having to make changes, however slight, encourages them to examine in more detail how a given implementation works.

COMBINING THE LABORATORIES WITH PROGRAMMING PROJECTS

One of my goals in designing these laboratories was to have students produce code in the laboratory that they use again as part of larger, more applications-oriented programming projects. The ADTs students develop in the Prelab exercises provide a solid foundation for such projects. Reusing the material that they created in laboratory frees students to focus on the applications they are developing. More important, they see in concrete terms—their time and effort—the value of such essential software engineering concepts as structured programming, data abstraction, and code reuse.

The second exercise in each In-lab is an applications problem based on the material covered in the Prelab for that laboratory. These exercises provide an excellent starting point for programming projects. Free-form projects are also possible. The PROJECTS directory on the Instructor's Disk contains a set of programming projects based on the ADTs developed in the laboratories.

STANDARD PASCAL

I have made every attempt to use standard Pascal throughout this manual and in the supporting software. The uses of nonstandard Pascal are summarized below.

- The ability to read from (or write to) a text data file is employed in the following exercises:
  Laboratory 1, In-lab Exercises 1 and 2
  Laboratory 6, In-lab Exercise 2
  Laboratory 7, In-lab Exercise 2
  Laboratory 10, In-lab Exercise 2
  Laboratory 11, In-lab Exercise 2
  Laboratory 14, In-lab Exercise 2
- A random number generator (uniform distribution) is used in the following exercises:
  Laboratory 5, In-lab Exercise 2
  Laboratory 12, In-lab Exercise 2
  Laboratory 15, In-lab Exercises 2 and 3

STUDENT DISK

Challenging students is easy; helping them to meet a challenge is not. The Student Disk packaged with the manual includes a set of software tools that assist students in developing ADT implementations. The tools provide students with the means for testing an implementation using simple keyboard commands and for visualizing the resulting data structure using ASCII text on a standard text display. Additional files containing data, partial solution shells, and other supporting routines are also included on this disk.

INSTRUCTOR'S DISK

An Instructor's Disk is available on request from D. C. Heath and Company. This disk contains solutions to all Prelab and In-lab exercises, as well as a set of programming projects compatible with the laboratories in this manual.

Acknowledgments

I would like to thank Susan Lilly for introducing me to the wonderful people at D. C. Heath and wish to give particular thanks to my editors, Randall Adams, Karen Myer, and Sarah Doyle. Their ideas and efforts transformed a utilitarian manuscript into a polished project.

I am also grateful to the following manuscript reviewers for their many insightful comments and suggestions: Harold C. Grossman, Clemson University; Linda Herndon, O.S.B., Benedictine College; Wayne B. Hewitt, Johnson County Community College; Herbert G. Mapes, Gallaudet University; Mary Dee Medley, Augusta College; Paul M. Mullins, Youngstown State University; James C. Pleasant, East Tennessee State University; Charles W. Reynolds, James Madison University.

My thanks also to Karen Nowicki, Shang Guo, and Sunil Nair for their comments on earlier drafts of these laboratories.

I especially wish to thank Bob Carlson, Charlie Bauer, and George Smith for their advice and encouragement. Finally, I owe a great debt of thanks to my wife Ruby for her patience and support.

J.R.

Contents

Token ADT

OVERVIEW

When computers were first introduced, they were popularly characterized as giant calculating machines. As you saw in your introductory programming course, this characterization ignored the fact that computers are equally adept at manipulating such nonnumeric information as alphanumeric character data.

Standard Pascal supports the manipulation of character data through the built-in data type CHAR and the associated operations for the input, output, assignment, and comparison of character data. Because we often need to manipulate characters in groups, or **strings**, rather than as individual characters, most contemporary dialects of Pascal have been extended to include a built-in string data type. In some dialects, the string data type is denoted as STRING[N], where N is an integer that specifies the maximum number of characters in a string. In other dialects, the string data type is denoted as CHAR[N] or VARYING[N] OF CHAR. Typically, the string data type has an associated set of operations that support the input, output, assignment, and comparison of strings, as well as operations that return the length of a string, a subset of a string, and the string produced by concatenating a pair of strings.

In this laboratory, you examine a still more sophisticated type of character data, the **delimited string**. Consider the following line of text.

```
LOAD DATABASE
```

When you read this line, you see two strings: 'LOAD' and 'DATABASE'. This is the result of our tendency to break text into delimited strings by using spaces as string delimiters.

Many programs require the ability to form and manipulate delimited strings. Depending on the program, these strings may be English words, user commands, symbols, or specialized keywords. For example, the command

```
DISPLAY LAST_NAME = Jones
```

might be used to direct a database program to display employee records for all employees named Jones. In order to process this command, the database program first must divide the command into the delimited strings

```
'DISPLAY'    'LAST_NAME'    '='    'Jones'
```

Once this division into strings has been accomplished, the program can execute the function the strings specify. Similarly, a Pascal compiler begins compilation of the statement

```
FOR J := 1 TO 5 DO WRITELN ;
```

by dividing the statement into the delimited strings

```
'FOR'   'J'   ':='   '1'   'TO'   '5'   'DO'   'WRITELN'   ';'
```

The term **token** is used in computer science to refer to a delimited string. Although the rules that define token delimiters tend to be somewhat problem-dependent, one common rule is to use blanks (spaces) to delimit tokens. Using this rule, we define a token to be a sequence of printable characters (possibly empty) that is bounded by blanks or by the end of a line of text. This definition forms the basis of a new data type called Token. In order to distinguish our new data type from Pascal's built-in data types, we refer to it as an **abstract data type**, or **ADT**.

When specifying an ADT, we first describe what type of **elements** constitute the ADT. Then we describe how these elements are put together, that is, the ADT's **structure**. In the case of the Token ADT, the elements are printable characters (excluding blanks) that are arranged to form a linearly ordered structure (that is, a string). Having specified the structure of the ADT, we then define how it can be used by specifying the associated **operations**. For each operation, we specify what conditions must be true before the operation can be applied (its preconditions or **requirements**) as well as what conditions will be true once the operation has been completed (its postconditions or **results**). The Token ADT specification that follows includes operations that support the input, output, and comparison of tokens.

TOKEN ADT

ELEMENTS
Any printable characters except blanks.

STRUCTURE
The characters in a token form a linear structure: the characters follow one after the other, from the beginning of the token (the first character) to the end of the token (the last character). The maximum number of characters is denoted by MaxTokenLength.

OPERATIONS

```
PROCEDURE TokenRead ( VAR InFile : TEXT;
                      VAR T : Token       )
```

Requires:
Text file InFile has been opened for input.

Results:
Reads the next token from the current line in InFile and returns it in token T. The token reading process begins by reading blanks until a nonblank character is read. This character is the first character in the token. The remainder of the token is then read character by character until a blank or the end of the line is reached. Only the first MaxTokenLength characters of any token are retained, but all characters in the token are read in. Any blanks encountered during the reading process are not part of the token and are *not* retained. Note that the TokenRead operation does not automatically move to the next line of text once it reaches the end of the current line. If there are no more tokens on the current line when TokenRead is called, T returns the empty token (the token that contains no characters).

```
PROCEDURE TokenWrite ( VAR OutFile : TEXT;
                            T : Token             )
```

Requires:
Text file OutFile has been opened for output, and T is a valid token.
Results:
Outputs T to OutFile. The symbol "<" is output immediately before T and the symbol ">" is output immediately after T. The TokenWrite operation does *not* advance to the next line after writing a token.

```
FUNCTION TokenMatch ( T1,
                      T2 : Token ) : BOOLEAN
```

Requires:
T1 and T2 are valid tokens.
Results:
Returns true if T1 is identical to T2. Otherwise, returns false.

We have defined the TokenRead operation in terms of the file variable InFile so it can be used to read tokens from either a text file or the keyboard. The following call reads a token from the text file associated with the file variable DataFile.

```
TokenRead(DataFile,NextToken);
```

By using the Pascal standard input file, you can read a token from the keyboard using the call

```
TokenRead(INPUT,NextToken);
```

You can use this same idea with the TokenWrite operation. In this case, you can write a token to a specified text file or else write to the Pascal standard output file to output a token to the screen.

LABORATORY 1: Cover Sheet

Date .... Section ....

Name ....

Place a check mark in the "Assigned" column next to the exercises your instructor has assigned to your class. Attach this cover sheet to the front of the packet of materials you submit following the laboratory.

	Assigned	*Completed*
Prelab Exercise	✓	
In-lab Exercise 1	✓	
In-lab Exercise 2		
In-lab Exercise 3		
In-lab Exercise 4		
Postlab Exercise 1		
Postlab Exercise 2		
		Total

LABORATORY 1: Prelab Exercise

Date .... Section ....

Name ....

Having completed the specification of the Token ADT, your next task is to implement the Token ADT operations in Pascal. You begin the implementation process by deciding how to represent a token. You then create a set of TYPE declarations that embody that representation.

The elements that form a token are all of type CHAR. Thus, it seems natural to represent a token as an array of characters. But, because tokens vary in length, you must store the length of the token along with the characters in the token. The result is the following TYPE declaration.

```
Token = RECORD
          Length : 0..MaxTokenLength;
          Ch     : ARRAY [ 1..MaxTokenLength ] OF CHAR;
        END;
```

Note that this declaration depends on the constant MaxTokenLength. You must specify the value of this constant in any program that uses the Token ADT. In this way, you can vary the amount of memory allocated to store a token from program to program. Within a given program, however, all tokens occupy the same amount of memory.

Step 1: Create a file called TOKEN.DEC that contains the TYPE declaration given above. Include comments that describe what a token is and what roles the Length and Ch fields play in this representation of a token.

Step 2: Now that you have chosen a token representation, use this representation to develop Pascal procedures and functions that implement the operations in the Token ADT. Note that each operation's specification includes the header for the corresponding procedure or function. The specification also describes what the operation does, including what inputs the operation expects and what outputs it produces. Create a Pascal implementation of the operations in the Token ADT using an array to store the characters in a token. Base your implementation on the TYPE declaration given above.

Step 3: Create a file called TOKEN.PAS that contains the routines in your implementation. For each routine, include comments that describe the corresponding operation.

The files TOKEN.DEC and TOKEN.PAS combine to form a Pascal implementation of the Token ADT. Your implementation is divided into two files because the syntax of Pascal dictates that declarations and routines be included at different points within a program. You must include the TYPE declaration in the file TOKEN.DEC as part of the program's TYPE declaration section and the routines in the file TOKEN.PAS after the program's VAR declaration section. The following program shows where to include these files in a program that uses the Token ADT.

```
PROGRAM TokenSample ( INPUT, OUTPUT );

{ Reads a token from the keyboard and outputs it.  }

CONST MaxTokenLength = 10;     { Specifies maximum token length  }

TYPE {  Include the TYPE declaration in the file TOKEN.DEC here.  }

VAR  InToken : Token;  {  Input token  }

{  Include the routines in the file TOKEN.PAS here.  }

BEGIN
WRITE('Enter token  : ');
TokenRead(INPUT,InToken);     READLN;
TokenWrite(OUTPUT,InToken);   WRITELN;
END.
```

Precisely how you include these files in a program depends on your programming environment. There are two common methods: using an editor and using an include directive. With the first method, you use the editor to insert the contents of the files TOKEN.DEC and TOKEN.PAS into the program while editing the program. This method is the more universal of the two; it works in almost any programming environment. However, this technique has a serious disadvantage. Should you need to change the Token ADT implementation—to correct a mistake, for instance—you will need to reinsert the updated files into every program that uses the Token ADT, a tedious task.

If your compiler supports an **include directive**, an alternative method is to use a pair of include directives to include the contents of the files TOKEN.DEC and TOKEN.PAS in the program. The form of the include directive varies from system to system. The following are typical include directives.

```
{$I Filename}            Turbo Pascal
%INCLUDE 'Filename'      VAX Pascal
```

An include directive instructs the compiler to compile the code in the specified file when it reaches the include directive in the program.

Let's look at an example. Note that this example uses the Turbo Pascal form of the include directive.

```
PROGRAM TokenSample ( INPUT, OUTPUT );

{ Reads a token from the keyboard and outputs it.  }

CONST MaxTokenLength = 10;     { Specifies maximum token length  }

TYPE {  Include the TYPE declaration in the file TOKEN.DEC here.  }
     {$I TOKEN.DEC}

VAR  InToken : Token;  {  Input token  }

{  Include the routines in the file TOKEN.PAS here.  }
{$I TOKEN.PAS}
```

```
BEGIN
WRITE('Enter token  : ');
TokenRead(INPUT,InToken);     READLN;
TokenWrite(OUTPUT,InToken);   WRITELN;
END.
```

The compiler begins compilation of this program by processing the PROGRAM and CONST declarations. When it reaches the include directive {$I TOKEN.DEC}, the compiler switches to file TOKEN.DEC and compiles the TYPE declaration contained in that file. Once it has finished compiling this declaration, the compiler switches back to the program and compiles the VAR declaration. Upon reaching the include directive {$I TOKEN.PAS}, the compiler switches to the file TOKEN.PAS and compiles the routines in that file. When it has completed these routines, it switches back to the program and finishes by compiling the executable portion of the program.

One benefit of using include directives is that you need to maintain only a single copy of the Token ADT (in the files TOKEN.DEC and TOKEN.PAS). In addition, the resulting program is shorter and easier to read.

LABORATORY 1: In-lab Exercise 1

Date .... Section ....

Name ....

Test your implementation of the Token ADT using the program in the file TEST1.PAS. This program supports the following tests.

Test	Action
1	Reads a token from the keyboard and outputs it to the screen.
2	Reads a pair of tokens from the keyboard and compares them.
3	Reads a set of token pairs from the file CMDSET.DAT and writes them to the file CMDTOKEN.DAT.

Step 1: Complete the following test plan by filling in the expected result for each input line.

Step 2: Execute this test plan. If you discover mistakes in your implementation of the Token ADT, correct them and execute the test plan again.

Test Plan for Test 1 (Token ADT)			
Test case	*Input line*	*Expected result*	*Checked*
Simple token	ABCDE		
Single-character token	A		
Symbols in token	#34@A		
Leading blanks	ABCDE		
Maximum length token	ABCDEFGHIJ		
Too long	ABCDEFGHIJKL		
Empty token			

Step 3: Complete the following test plan by filling in the expected result for each pair of tokens.

Step 4:   Execute this test plan. If you discover mistakes in your implementation of the TokenMatch operation, correct them and execute the test plan again.

Test Plan for Test 2 (Token ADT)			
Test case	*Pair of tokens*	*Expected result*	*Checked*
Identical tokens	ABCDE ABCDE		
Different characters	ABCDE 12345		
Different lengths	ABCDE ABC		
Identical character	1 1		
Different character	1 A		
One token empty	ABC		
Both tokens empty			
Maximum length match	ABCDEFGHIJ ABCDEFGHIJ		
Maximum length different	ABCDEFGHIJ ABCDEFG123		

Step 5:   Test 3 uses the operations in the Token ADT to divide the command lines in the file CMDSET.DAT into tokens and writes the results to the file CMDTOKEN.DAT. Complete the following test plan by filling in the expected result for each line in CMDSET.DAT.

Step 6:   Execute this test plan. If you discover mistakes in your implementation of the Token ADT, correct them and execute the test plan again.

Test Plan for Test 3 (Token ADT)		
Contents of CMDSET.DAT	*Expected result*	*Checked*
ADD KEYWORD DELETE 1 1 2 SKIP3 32 TRUE THISTOKENISTOOLONG CUT		

LABORATORY 1: In-lab Exercise 2

Date .... Section ....

Name ....

As we noted in the Pre-lab exercise, a compiler begins the compilation process by breaking a program down into tokens. This process is referred to as **lexical analysis**.

Step 1: Create a Pascal program that performs lexical analysis on a text file containing a Pascal program. Your program should read the tokens in the file and output each token to the screen using the following format.

```
1 : <1stToken>
2 : <2ndToken>
      ...
```

This format requires that your program maintain a running count of the number of tokens that have been read from the text file. You may assume that the tokens in the text file are delimited by blanks or by the ends of lines, an assumption that is not true for Pascal programs in general.

Your lexical analysis program should manipulate tokens using the operations in the Token ADT. It should *not* include references similar to the following.

```
InToken.Ch[J]    or    NewToken.Length
```

Step 2: Test your lexical analysis program using the text file PROGSAMP.DAT. The contents of this file are shown below.

```
PROGRAM Sample ( OUTPUT ) ;

VAR J : INTEGER ;

BEGIN
FOR J := 1 TO 20 DO
    WRITE ( J : 2 ) ;
END .
```

LABORATORY 1: In-lab Exercise 3

Date .... Section ....

Name ....

Concatenation is a useful operation for any string data type, including the Token ADT. An operation for concatenating tokens is described below.

```
PROCEDURE TokenConcatenate ( VAR TBase : Token;
                                 TAdd  : Token  )
```

Requires:
Tokens TBase and TAdd are valid tokens.

Results:
Appends TAdd to the end of TBase. Only appends as many characters from TAdd as can be added without exceeding the size limits on a token.

Step 1:   Create a Pascal implementation of this operation.

Step 2:   Add your implementation of this operation to the file TOKEN.PAS.

Step 3:   Add the following code to the test program in the file TEST1.PAS.

```
TokenConcatenate(InToken1,InToken2);
TokenWrite(OUTPUT,InToken1);
```

Step 4:   Complete the following test plan by filling in the expected result for each pair of tokens.

Step 5:   Execute this test plan. If you discover mistakes in your implementation of the TokenConcatenate operation, correct them and execute the test plan again.

Test Plan for the TokenConcatenate operation			
Test case	*Pair of tokens*	*Expected result*	*Checked*
Simple tokens	ABCD 1234		
Different lengths	ABCD 123		
TBase empty	123		
TAdd empty	ABC		
Both empty			
Combined length greater than MaxTokenLength	ABCDEF 123456		

LABORATORY 1: In-lab Exercise 4

Date .... Section ....

Name ....

Your programs frequently will need to manipulate tokens that denote numerical values. The Token ADT operations described below assist in processing tokens that can be interpreted as nonnegative integers.

FUNCTION TokenIsNumeric (T : Token) : BOOLEAN

Requires:
T is a valid token.
Results:
Returns true if T contains only the characters '0'..'9', that is, if T corresponds to a nonnegative integer. Otherwise, returns false.

FUNCTION TokenNumericValue (T : Token) : INTEGER

Requires:
Token T corresponds to a nonnegative integer.
Results:
Returns the integer value corresponding to T.

Step 1: Create Pascal implementations of these operations.

Step 2: Add your implementation of these operations to the file TOKEN.PAS.

 Step 3: Add the following code to the test program in the file TEST1.PAS.

```
IF TokenIsNumeric(InToken1)
   THEN WRITELN('Integer value is',
                TokenNumericValue(InToken1))
   ELSE WRITELN('Token is NOT a nonnegative integer');
```

Step 4: Complete the following test plan by filling in the expected result for each token.

Step 5: Execute the test plan. If you discover mistakes in your implementation of these operations, correct them and execute the test plan again.

Test Plan for the TokenIsNumeric and TokenNumericValue operations			
Test case	*Token*	*Expected result*	*Checked*
Positive integer	12		
Large integer value	1470		
One	1		
Zero	0		
Real number	3.1415		
Negative integer	−321		

LABORATORY 1: Postlab Exercise 1

Date .... Section ....

Name ....

PART A

Rather than explicitly storing the number of characters in a token, we could have marked the end of a token by placing a *special character* in the array immediately after the last character in the token. Show the modifications you would need to make to the TYPE declaration for type Token in order to support this approach. Briefly explain your modifications.

```
Token = RECORD




                END;
```

PART B

What character would you use as the special character? Why would you use this particular character?

LABORATORY 1: Postlab Exercise 2

Date .... Section ....

Name ....

PART A

Create another operation for the Token ADT and give its specification below. Simply define the operation; you need not implement it.

Requires:

Results:

PART B

Describe a problem in which you might use your new operation.

List ADT I

OVERVIEW

The list is one of the most commonly used data structures. Although all programs employ the same basic definition of a **list**—a sequence of homogeneous elements—the type of element stored in a list varies from program to program. Some use lists of integers, others use lists of characters, and so forth.

Rather than create a different list implementation for each type of list, you will create a single list implementation using list elements of some **generic** (or unspecified) type. You can customize this generic list implementation to produce any list you require simply by specifying this generic type.

For example, in the List ADT specification given below, we define a list in terms of elements of generic type ListElement. Once you have created an implementation of this generic List ADT, you can adapt your implementation to manipulate a list of integers by defining type ListElement to be equivalent to type INTEGER, using the following TYPE declaration.

```
TYPE ListElement = INTEGER;
```

Similarly, declaring type ListElement to be equivalent to type CHAR allows you to use your implementation to manipulate a list of characters.

LIST ADT

ELEMENTS
The elements in a list are of generic type ListElement.

STRUCTURE
The elements in a list form a linear structure; that is, the list elements follow one after the other, from the beginning of the list (the first element) to the end of the list (the last element). The order of the list elements is determined by when and where each element is inserted and is *not* a function of the data contained in the list elements.

At any point, one element in any nonempty list is designated as the **current list element**. Insertions and deletions are made relative to the current list element. You can travel through the list by changing this designation.

OPERATIONS

PROCEDURE ListCreate (VAR L : List)

Requires:
None.
Results:
Creates an empty list L.

PROCEDURE ListInsert (VAR L : List;
NewElement : ListElement)

Requires:
List L is not full.
Results:
Inserts list element NewElement into L. If L is not empty, then NewElement is inserted immediately after the current list element. Otherwise, NewElement is inserted as the first (and only) element in L. In either case, NewElement becomes the current list element.

PROCEDURE ListDelete (VAR L : List)

Requires:
List L is not empty.
Results:
Deletes the current list element from L. If the resulting list is not empty, then the element that followed the deleted element becomes the current list element. If the deleted element was at the end of the list, then the first element in the list becomes the current list element.

PROCEDURE ListCurrent (L : List;
VAR CurrentElement : ListElement)

Requires:
List L is not empty.
Results:
CurrentElement returns a copy of the current list element.

PROCEDURE ListReplace (VAR L : List;
NewElement : ListElement)

Requires:
List L is not empty.
Results:
Replaces the current list element with list element NewElement.

PROCEDURE ListGotoNext (VAR L : List)

Requires:
List L is not empty, and the current list element is not at the end of L.
Results:
The element immediately after the current list element becomes the current list element.

PROCEDURE ListGotoPrior (VAR L : List)

Requires:
List L is not empty, and the current list element is not at the beginning of L.
Results:
The element immediately before the current list element becomes the current list element.

PROCEDURE ListGotoBeginning (VAR L : List)

Requires:
List L is not empty.
Results:
The element at the beginning of L becomes the current list element.

PROCEDURE ListGotoEnd (VAR L : List)

Requires:
List L is not empty.
Results:
The element at the end of L becomes the current list element.

FUNCTION ListEmpty (L : List) : BOOLEAN

Requires:
List L has been created.
Results:
If L is empty, then returns true. Otherwise, returns false.

FUNCTION ListFull (L : List) : BOOLEAN

Requires:
List L has been created.
Results:
If L is full, then returns true. Otherwise, returns false.

FUNCTION ListAtBeginning (L : List) : BOOLEAN

Requires:
List L is not empty.
Results:
If the current list element is at the beginning of L, then returns true. Otherwise, returns false.

FUNCTION ListAtEnd (L : List) : BOOLEAN

Requires:
List L is not empty.
Results:
If the current list element is at the end of L, then returns true. Otherwise, returns false.

PROCEDURE ListClear (VAR L : List)

Requires:
List L has been created.
Results:
Deletes all elements in L.

PROCEDURE ListShowStructure (L : List)

Requires:
List L has been created.
Results:
Outputs the elements in L. If L is empty, outputs "Empty list". This operation is intended for debugging purposes only. It violates the principle of data abstraction by assuming that list elements can be output using a WRITE statement.

LABORATORY 2: Cover Sheet

Date .... Section ....

Name ....

Place a check mark in the "Assigned" column next to the exercises your instructor has assigned to your class. Attach this cover sheet to the front of the packet of materials you submit following the laboratory.

	Assigned	*Completed*
Prelab Exercise	✓	
In-lab Exercise 1	✓	
In-lab Exercise 2		
In-lab Exercise 3		
In-lab Exercise 4		
Postlab Exercise 1		
Postlab Exercise 2		
		Total

LABORATORY 2: Prelab Exercise

Date .... Section ....

Name ....

You can implement a list in many ways. Given that all elements in a list are of the same type (ListElement) and that the list itself is linear, an array composed of elements of type ListElement seems a natural choice.

Step 1: Create a Pascal implementation of the List ADT using an array to store the list elements. Because the list will change in size, you need to store the number of elements in the list (Size), along with the list elements themselves (Element). You also need to store the array index of the current list element (Current). Base your implementation on the following TYPE declaration.

```
List = RECORD
         Size,
         Current : 0..MaxListArraySize;
         Element : ARRAY [ 1..MaxListArraySize ] OF ListElement;
       END;
```

A CONST declaration defining MaxListArraySize and a TYPE declaration defining ListElement must appear in any program that uses this implementation of the List ADT. For example, you can use the following code fragment to declare a list of integers, NumList, that contains at most ten integers.

```
CONST MaxListArraySize = 10;

TYPE ListElement = INTEGER;
     { Include the TYPE declaration for the array  }
     { implementation of the List ADT here.        }

VAR  NumList : List;

{ Include the routines in the array implementation  }
{ of the List ADT here.                             }
```

Note that an implementation of the ListShowStructure operation is given in the file SHOW2.PAS.

Step 2: Create a file called LISTARR.DEC that contains the TYPE declaration for type List and a file called LISTARR.PAS that contains the routines in your implementation. Include comments that describe the array representation of a list and the operations in your implementation.

LABORATORY 2: In-lab Exercise 1

Date .... Section ....

Name ....

In this and subsequent laboratories, you will use interactive, command-driven test programs to evaluate your ADT implementations. Using this kind of test program, you can check a test case by simply entering a sequence of keyboard commands and observing the results.

The test program in the file TEST2.PAS allows you to interactively test your implementation of the List ADT using the following commands.

Command	Action
+x	Insert element x.
–	Delete the current list element.
@	Get the current list element and output it.
=x	Replace the current list element with element x.
N	Go to the next list element.
P	Go to the prior list element.
<	Go to the beginning of the list.
>	Go to the end of the list.
E	Report whether the list is empty.
F	Report whether the list is full.
[	Report whether the current list element is at the beginning of the list.
]	Report whether the current list element is at the end of the list.
C	Clear the list.
Q	Quit the test program.

Suppose you wish to confirm that your implementation of the List ADT will successfully insert an element into a list that has been emptied by a series of calls to the ListDelete operation. You can test this case by entering the following sequence of keyboard commands.

Command	+a	+b	–	–	+c	Q
Action	Insert a	Insert b	Delete b	Delete a	Insert c	Exit

Although an interactive test program allows you to rapidly examine a variety of test cases, you must be careful not to violate the preconditions required by the operations you are testing. For instance, the commands

Command	+a	+b	–	–	–
Action	Insert **a**	Insert **b**	Delete **b**	Delete **a**	Error

will cause the test program to fail during the last call to the ListDelete operation. The source of this failure does not lie in the implementation of the List ADT, nor is the test program flawed. This failure results from a sequence of commands that violate the preconditions of the ListDelete operation (the list must *not* be empty when ListDelete is invoked). The very advantage of an interactive, command-driven test program—its speed—makes it easy to make mistakes such as this one. It is very tempting to just sit down and start entering commands. A better strategy, however, is to create a test plan listing the test cases you wish to check and then to write out command sequences that generate these test cases.

Step 1: Complete the following test plan by adding test cases that check whether your implementation of the List ADT correctly processes insertions into a newly emptied list, insertions that fill a list to its maximum size, deletions from a full list, and calls to the ListEmpty and ListFull operations. Assume that the output of one test case is used as the input to the following test case. Note that although expected results are listed for the final command in each command sequence, you should confirm that *every* command produces a correct result. The current list element is shown in bold.

Step 2: Execute your test plan. If you discover mistakes in your implementation of the List ADT, correct them and execute your test plan again.

Step 3: Change type ListElement to INTEGER in the test program, and replace the character data ('a'–'g') in your test plan with numeric values.

Step 4: Execute your revised test plan using the revised test program. If you discover mistakes in your implementation of the List ADT, correct them and execute your revised test plan again.

Test Plan for the operations in the List ADT			
Test case	*Commands*	*Expected result*	*Checked*
Insert at end	+a +b +c +d	a b c **d**	
Travel from beginning	< N N	a b **c** d	
Travel from end	> P P	a **b** c d	
Delete middle element	–	a **c** d	
Insert in middle	+e +f +f	a c e f **f** d	
Delete last element	> –	a c e f **f**	
Delete first element	–	**c** e f f	
Get current element	@	Returns **c**	
Replace current element	=g	**g** e f f	
At the beginning?	[N [> [	True False False	
At the end?	] P] <]	True False False	
Clear list	C	Empty list	

LABORATORY 2: In-lab Exercise 2

Date .... Section ....

Name ....

The genetic information encoded in a strand of deoxyribonucleic acid (DNA) is stored using the purine and pyrimidine bases adenine, guanine, cytosine, and thymine. Biologists often are interested not only in the pattern of bases in a given DNA sequence, but also in the number of times each base occurs in the sequence.

By representing a DNA sequence as a list containing occurrences of the characters 'A', 'G', 'C', and 'T', you can use your implementation of the List ADT to develop the following procedure.

```
PROCEDURE CountBases ( DNASequence : List;
                       VAR ACount, GCount,
                           CCount, TCount : INTEGER )
```

Inputs:
DNASequence contains the bases in a DNA strand. These bases are encoded using the characters 'A', 'C', 'T', and 'G'.

Outputs:
ACount, GCount, CCount, and TCount return the number of times the corresponding character (base) appears in the DNA sequence.

Step 1:   Create a Pascal implementation of this procedure. Your procedure should manipulate the DNA sequence using the operations in the List ADT. It should *not* include references such as the following.

       DNASequence.Current   or   DNASequence.Element [J]

Step 2:   Create a file called DNACOUNT.PAS that contains your implementation of the CountBases procedure.

Step 3:   Before testing your implementation of this procedure using the test program in the file TEST2DNA.PAS, complete the following test plan. Include DNA sequences of different lengths and various combinations of bases.

Step 4:   Execute your test plan. If you discover mistakes in your implementation of the CountBases procedure, correct them and execute your test plan again.

| Test Plan for the CountBases procedure ||||
Test case	DNA sequence	Expected result	Checked
Sequence with 10 bases	AGTACATGTA	ACount = 4 GCount = 2 CCount = 1 TCount = 3	

LABORATORY 2: In-lab Exercise 3

Date .... Section ....

Name ....

In many applications of lists, you need to be able to reorganize the lists elements. An operation for changing the order of the elements in a list is described below.

```
PROCEDURE ListMoveToNth ( VAR L : List;
                              N : INTEGER   )
```

Requires:
List L contains at least N elements.

Results:
Removes the current list element from L and reinserts it as Nth element in L (counting from the beginning of L). This element remains the current list element.

Step 1:   Create a Pascal implementation of this operation.

Step 2:   Add your implementation of this operation to the file LISTARR.PAS.

Step 3:   Add the following code to the test program in the file TEST2.PAS.

```
ELSE IF ( Cmd = 'M' ) OR ( Cmd = 'm' )
   THEN BEGIN
        ListMoveToNth(TestList,N);
        WRITELN('Current element moved to position ',N);
        END
```

You also must change the statement

```
IF ( Cmd = '+' ) OR ( Cmd = '=' )
   THEN READLN(TestElement)
   ELSE READLN;
```

to the statement

```
IF ( Cmd = '+' ) OR ( Cmd = '=' )
   THEN READLN(TestElement)
ELSE IF ( Cmd = 'M' ) OR ( Cmd = 'm' )
   THEN READLN(N)
ELSE READLN;
```

so you can specify the position to which the current list element is to be moved. Variable N is of type INTEGER.

Step 4:   Complete the following test plan by adding test cases that check whether your implementation of the ListMoveToNth operation correctly processes moves within full and single-element lists.

Step 5: Execute your test plan. If you discover mistakes in your implementation of the ListMoveToNth operation, correct them and execute your test plan again.

Test Plan for the ListMoveToNth operation			
Test case	*Commands*	*Expected result*	*Checked*
Set up list	+a +b +c +d	a b c **d**	
Move first element	< M3	b c **a** d	
Move element back	M1	**a** b c d	
Move to end of list	M4	b c d **a**	
Move back one	M3	b c **a** d	
Move forward one	M4	b c d **a**	

LABORATORY 2: In-lab Exercise 4

Date .... Section ....

Name ....

Using the ListGotoNext operation to travel element-by-element through a list is a tedious way to locate an element in a long list. An operation that searches for a specified list element is described below.

```
FUNCTION ListSearch ( VAR L : List;
                      SrchElement : ListElement ) : BOOLEAN
```

Requires:
List L has been created.
Results:
Searches the elements in list L for SrchElement. The search begins with the *current list element* and progresses to the end of the list (if necessary). If SrchElement is found, then that occurrence of SrchElement becomes the current list element and ListSearch returns true. Otherwise, ListSearch returns false and the current list element designation remains unchanged.

Step 1: Create a Pascal implementation of this operation.

Step 2: Add your implementation of this operation to the file LISTARR.PAS.

 Step 3: Add the following code to the test program in the file TEST2.PAS.

```
ELSE IF Cmd = '?'
    THEN IF ListSearch(TestList,TestElement)
            THEN WRITELN('Found')
            ELSE WRITELN('Not found')
```

You also must change the statement

```
IF ( Cmd = '+' ) OR ( Cmd = '=' )
    THEN READLN(TestElement)
    ELSE READLN;
```

to the statement

```
IF ( Cmd = '+' ) OR ( Cmd = '=' ) OR ( Cmd = '?' )
    THEN READLN(TestElement)
    ELSE READLN;
```

so you can specify the element to search for.

Step 4: Complete the following test plan by adding test cases that check whether your implementation of the ListSearch operation correctly conducts searches in empty and full lists, as well as searches that begin with the last element in a list.

Step 5:   Execute your test plan. If you discover mistakes in your implementation of the ListSearch operation, correct them and execute your test plan again.

Test Plan for the ListSearch operation			
Test case	*Commands*	*Expected result*	*Checked*
Set up list	+a +b +c +a	a b c **a**	
Successful search	< ?a	Search succeeds **a** b c a	
Search for duplicate	N ?a	Search succeeds a b c **a**	
Successful search	< ?b	Search succeeds a **b** c d	
Search for duplicate	N ?b	Search fails a b **c** a	
Trivial search	?c	Search succeeds a b **c** a	

LABORATORY 2: Postlab Exercise 1

Date .... Section ....

Name ....

Given a list containing N elements, develop worst-case, order-of-magnitude estimates of the execution time of the following List ADT operations, assuming they are implemented using an array. Briefly explain your reasoning behind each estimate.

ListInsert	O( )

Explanation:

ListDelete	O( )

Explanation:

ListGotoNext   O(   )

Explanation:

ListGotoPrior   O(   )

Explanation:

LABORATORY 2: Postlab Exercise 2

Date .... Section ....

Name ....

PART A

Give the declarations (CONST, TYPE, and VAR) that are needed in order to declare a variable, Samples, to be a list of real numbers. Assume that Samples will contain no more than 50 real numbers.

PART B

Give the declarations (CONST, TYPE, and VAR) that are needed in order to declare a variable, Coords, to be a list of (X,Y)-coordinate pairs, where X and Y are real numbers. Assume that Coords will contain no more than 20 (X,Y)-coordinate pairs.

PART C

Are the declarations that you created in Parts A and B compatible with the operations in your implementation of the List ADT? Briefly explain why or why not.

List ADT II

OVERVIEW

Multiple implementations of an ADT are necessary if the ADT is to perform efficiently in a variety of operating environments. Depending on the hardware and the application, you may want an implementation that reduces the execution time of some (or all) of the ADT operations, or you may want an implementation that reduces the amount of memory needed to store the ADT elements.

In Laboratory 2, you created an implementation of the List ADT using an array to store the list elements. The resulting implementation forced you to determine the size of a list at compile time. In addition, each insertion and deletion required shifting list elements within the array.

In this laboratory, you create an implementation of the List ADT based on a singly linked list. This implementation allocates memory for elements as they are inserted into the list. Equally important, a linked list can be reconfigured following an insertion or deletion simply by changing one or two links.

LIST ADT

ELEMENTS
The elements in a list are of generic type ListElement.

STRUCTURE
The elements in a list form a linear structure; that is, the list elements follow one after the other, from the beginning of the list (the first element) to the end of the list (the last element). The order of the list elements is determined by when and where each element is inserted, and is *not* a function of the data contained in the list elements.

At any point, one element in any nonempty list is designated as the **current list element**. Insertions and deletions are made relative to the current list element. You can travel through the list by changing this designation.

OPERATIONS

PROCEDURE ListCreate (VAR L : List)

Requires:
None
Results:
Creates an empty list L.

PROCEDURE ListInsert (VAR L : List;
                        NewElement : ListElement)

Requires:
List L is not full.
Results:
Inserts list element NewElement into L. If L is not empty, then NewElement is inserted immediately after the current list element. Otherwise, NewElement is inserted as the first (and only) element in L. In either case, NewElement becomes the current list element.

PROCEDURE ListDelete (VAR L : List)

Requires:
List L is not empty.
Results:
Deletes the current list element from L. If the resulting list is not empty, then the element that followed the deleted element becomes the current list element. If the deleted element was at the end of the list, then the first element in the list becomes the current list element.

PROCEDURE ListCurrent (L : List;
                        VAR CurrentElement : ListElement)

Requires:
List L is not empty.
Results:
CurrentElement returns a copy of the current list element.

PROCEDURE ListReplace (VAR L : List;
                        NewElement : ListElement)

Requires:
List L is not empty.
Results:
Replaces the current list element with list element NewElement.

PROCEDURE ListGotoNext (VAR L : List)

Requires:
List L is not empty, and the current list element is not at the end of L.
Results:
The element immediately after the current list element becomes the current list element.

PROCEDURE ListGotoPrior (VAR L : List)

Requires:
List L is not empty, and the current list element is not at the beginning of L.
Results:
The element immediately before the current list element becomes the current list element.

PROCEDURE ListGotoBeginning (VAR L : List)

Requires:
List L is not empty.
Results:
The element at the beginning of L becomes the current list element.

PROCEDURE ListGotoEnd (VAR L : List)

Requires:
List L is not empty.
Results:
The element at the end of L becomes the current list element.

FUNCTION ListEmpty (L : List) : BOOLEAN

Requires:
List L has been created.
Results:
If L is empty, then returns true. Otherwise, returns false.

FUNCTION ListFull (L : List) : BOOLEAN

Requires:
List L has been created.
Results:
If L is full, then returns true. Otherwise, returns false.

FUNCTION ListAtBeginning (L : List) : BOOLEAN

Requires:
List L is not empty.
Results:
If the current list element is at the beginning of L, then returns true. Otherwise, returns false.

FUNCTION ListAtEnd (L : List) : BOOLEAN

Requires:
List L is not empty.
Results:
If the current list element is at the end of L, then returns true. Otherwise, returns false.

PROCEDURE ListClear (VAR L : List)

Requires:
List L has been created.
Results:
Deletes all elements in L.

PROCEDURE ListShowStructure (L : List)

Requires:
List L has been created.
Results:
Outputs the elements in L. If L is empty, outputs "Empty list". This operation is intended for debugging purposes only. It violates the principle of data abstraction by assuming that list elements can be output using a WRITE statement.

LABORATORY 3: Cover Sheet

Date .... Section ....

Name ....

Place a check mark in the "Assigned" column next to the exercises your instructor has assigned to your class. Attach this cover sheet to the front of the packet of materials you submit following the laboratory.

	Assigned	*Completed*
Prelab Exercise	✓	
In-lab Exercise 1	✓	
In-lab Exercise 2		
In-lab Exercise 3		
In-lab Exercise 4		
Postlab Exercise 1		
Postlab Exercise 2		
		Total

LABORATORY 3: Prelab Exercise

Date .... Section ....

Name ....

Step 1:   Create a Pascal implementation of the List ADT using a singly linked list to store the list elements. Each node in the linked list should contain a list element (Element) and a pointer to the node containing the next element in the list (Next). Your implementation should maintain pointers to the first node in the list (Head) and the node containing the current list element (Current). Base your implementation on the following TYPE declarations.

```
ListNodePtr = ^ListNode;

ListNode    = RECORD
                  Element : ListElement;
                  Next    : ListNodePtr;
              END;

List        = RECORD
                  Head,
                  Current : ListNodePtr;
              END;
```

Note that you must declare type ListElement in any program that uses the List ADT.

An implementation of the ListShowStructure operation is given in the file SHOW3.PAS.

Step 2:   Create a file called LISTLNK.DEC that contains the TYPE declarations given above and a file called LISTLNK.PAS that contains the routines in your implementation. Include comments that describe the linked list representation of a list and the operations in your implementation.

LABORATORY 3: In-lab Exercise 1

Date .... Section ....

Name ....

 The test program in the file TEST3.PAS allows you to interactively test your implementation of the List ADT using the following commands.

Command	Action
+x	Insert element x.
–	Delete the current list element.
@	Get the current list element and output it.
=x	Replace the current list element with element x.
N	Go to the next list element.
P	Go to the prior list element.
<	Go to the beginning of the list.
>	Go to the end of the list.
E	Report whether the list is empty.
F	Report whether the list is full.
[	Report whether the current list element is at the beginning of the list.
]	Report whether the current list element is at the end of the list.
C	Clear the list.
Q	Quit the test program.

Step 1: Complete the following test plan by adding test cases that check whether your implementation of the List ADT correctly processes insertions into a newly emptied list, and correctly executes calls to the ListEmpty operation. Assume that the output of one test case is used as the input to the following test case. Note that although expected results are listed for the final command in each command sequence, you should confirm that *every* command produces a correct result. The current list element is shown in bold.

Step 2: Execute your test plan. If you discover mistakes in your implementation of the List ADT, correct them and execute your test plan again.

Step 3:   Change type ListElement to INTEGER in the test program, and replace the character data ('a'–'g') in your test plan with numeric values.

Step 4:   Execute your revised test plan using the revised test program. If you discover mistakes in your implementation of the List ADT, correct them and execute your revised test plan again.

Test Plan for the operations in the List ADT			
Test case	*Commands*	*Expected result*	*Checked*
Insert at end	+a +b +c +d	a b c **d**	
Travel from beginning	< N N	a b **c** d	
Travel from end	> P P	a **b** c d	
Delete middle element	–	a c d	
Insert in middle	+e +f +f	a c e f **f** d	
Delete last element	> –	a c e f f	
Delete first element	–	c e f f	
Get current element	@	Returns **c**	
Replace current element	=g	**g** e f f	
At the beginning?	[N [> [	True False False	
At the end?	] P] <]	True False False	
Clear list	C	Empty list	

LABORATORY 3: In-lab Exercise 2

A string of characters can be represented in many ways. In Laboratory 1, you used an array of characters to represent a string. Alternatively, you can represent a string as a list of characters.

Step 1: Create a Pascal implementation of the following procedure.

PROCEDURE StringCapitalize (VAR Str : List)

Inputs:
Character string Str is not empty.
Outputs:
Replaces each lowercase letter in Str with the corresponding uppercase letter.

Your procedure should manipulate string Str using the operations in the List ADT. It should *not* include references such as the following.

```
Str.Current^.Element    or    Str.Head^.Element
```

Step 2: Create a file called STRCAP.PAS that contains your implementation of the StringCapitalize procedure.

Step 3: Before testing your implementation of this procedure using the test program in the file TEST3CAP.PAS, complete the following test plan. Include strings of different lengths that are composed of various combinations of lowercase and uppercase characters.

Step 4: Execute your test plan. If you discover mistakes in your implementation of the StringCapitalize procedure, correct them and execute your test plan again.

Test Plan for the StringCapitalize procedure			
Test case	*String*	*Expected result*	*Checked*
All lowercase characters	abcdefghij	ABCDEFGHIJ	

LABORATORY 3: In-lab Exercise 3

Date .... Section ....

Name ....

In many applications of lists, you need to be able to reorganize the lists elements. An operation for changing the order of the elements in a list is described below.

```
PROCEDURE ListMoveToFirst ( VAR L : List )
```

Requires:
List L is not empty.
Results:
Removes the current list element from L and reinserts at the beginning of L. This element remains the current list element.

Step 1:   Create a Pascal implementation of this operation.

Step 2:   Add your implementation of this operation to the file LISTLNK.PAS.

Step 3:   Add the following code to the test program in the file TEST3.PAS.

```
ELSE IF ( Cmd = 'M' ) OR ( Cmd = 'm' )
   THEN BEGIN
         WRITELN('Current element moved to ',
                 'beginning of list');
         ListMoveToFirst(TestList);
         END
```

Step 4:   Complete the following test plan by adding test cases that check whether your implementation of the ListMoveToFirst operation correctly processes attempts to move the first element in a list, as well as moves within a single element list.

Step 5:   Execute your test plan. If you discover mistakes in your implementation of the ListMoveToFirst operation, correct them and execute your test plan again.

Test Plan for the ListMoveToFirst operation			
Test case	*Commands*	*Expected result*	*Checked*
Set up list	+a +b +c +d	a b c **d**	
Move last element	M	**d** a b c	
Move second element	N M	a **d** b c	
Move third element	N N M	**b** a d c	

LABORATORY 3: In-lab Exercise 4

Date .... Section ....

Name ....

Your implementation of the List ADT allows you to determine what the current list element is, but not where it is in the list. An operation for determining the position of the current list element is described below.

FUNCTION ListPosition (L : List) : BOOLEAN

Requires:
List L is not empty.
Results:
Returns the position of the current list element, where the first element in L occupies position 1, the second element occupies position 2, and so forth.

Step 1: Create a Pascal implementation of this operation.

Step 2: Add your implementation of this operation to the file LISTLNK.PAS.

Step 3: Add the following code to the test program in the file TEST3.PAS.

```
ELSE IF Cmd = '#'
    THEN WRITELN('Current element is in position ',
                 ListPosition(TestList))
```

Step 4: Complete the following test plan by adding test cases that check whether your implementation of the ListPosition operation correctly determines the position of elements in lists that have had elements deleted, including lists that have been reduced to a single element.

Step 5: Execute your test plan. If you discover mistakes in your implementation of the ListPosition operation, correct them and execute your test plan again.

Test Plan for the ListPosition operation			
Test case	*Commands*	*Expected result*	*Checked*
Set up list	+a +b +c +d	a b c **d**	
First element	∠ #	Position 1	
Second element	N #	Position 2	
Third element	N #	Position 3	
Fourth element	N #	Position 4	

LABORATORY 3: Postlab Exercise 1

Date .... Section ....

Name ....

Given a list containing N elements, develop worst-case, order-of-magnitude estimates of the execution time of the following List ADT operations, assuming they are implemented using a singly linked list. Briefly explain your reasoning behind each estimate.

ListInsert   O(   )

Explanation:

ListDelete   O(   )

Explanation:

ListGotoNext   O(   )

Explanation:

ListGotoPrior   O(   )

Explanation:

LABORATORY 3: Postlab Exercise 2

Date .... Section ....

Name ....

Sometimes a more effective approach to a problem can be found by looking at the problem a little differently. Consider the following List ADT operation.

```
PROCEDURE ListInsertBefore ( VAR L : List;
                             NewElement : ListElement )
```

Requires:
List L is neither empty, nor full.
Results:
Inserts list element NewElement into L immediately before the current list element.

You can implement this operation using a singly linked list in two very different ways. With the first approach, you search through the list, beginning with the first list node. Once you reach the node immediately before the current list node, you insert a new node containing NewElement into the list between this node and the current list node. A more effective approach is to insert an empty node into the list immediately after the current list node. You then copy the data in the current list node into this new node and replace the data in the current list node with NewElement.

PART A

Why is the second approach more efficient than the first?

PART B

How might you apply the reasoning used in the second approach to the ListDelete operation?

Stack ADT

OVERVIEW

Many applications that use a linear data structure do not require the full complement of operations supported by the List ADT. Although it is possible to develop these applications using the List ADT, you may wish instead to define additional linear data structures whose operations more closely match the needs of these applications. By carefully defining the operations these data structures support, you can produce ADTs that meet the needs of a broad range of applications, but yield implementations that are more efficient (if narrower) than any implementation of the List ADT.

Consider the stack data structure, for instance. A **stack** is a linear data structure in which the elements are ordered from most recently added to least recently added. Only the most recently added stack element may be referenced directly, and examining this element entails removing it from the stack. The result is the "last in, first out" behavior that characterizes a stack. Although this data structure is narrowly defined, it is so extensively used by systems software that support for a primitive stack is one of the basic elements of most computer architectures.

STACK ADT

ELEMENTS
The elements in a stack are of generic type StackElement.

STRUCTURE
The stack elements are ordered linearly from most recently added (the top) to least recently added (the bottom). Elements are inserted (pushed) onto and removed (popped) from the top of the stack.

OPERATIONS

PROCEDURE StackCreate (VAR S : Stack)

Requires:
None.
Results:
Creates an empty stack S.

```
PROCEDURE Push ( VAR S : Stack;
                 NewElement : StackElement )
```

Requires:
Stack S is not full.
Results:
Inserts stack element NewElement onto the top of S.

```
PROCEDURE Pop ( VAR S : Stack;
                VAR TopElement : StackElement )
```

Requires:
Stack S is not empty.
Results:
Removes the most recently added (top) stack element from S and returns it in TopElement.

```
FUNCTION StackEmpty ( S : Stack ) : BOOLEAN
```

Requires:
Stack S has been created.
Results:
If S is empty, then returns true. Otherwise, returns false.

```
FUNCTION StackFull ( S : Stack ) : BOOLEAN
```

Requires:
Stack S has been created.
Results:
If S is full, then returns true. Otherwise, returns false.

```
PROCEDURE StackClear ( VAR S : Stack )
```

Requires:
Stack S has been created.
Results:
Deletes all elements in S.

```
PROCEDURE StackShowStructure ( S : Stack )
```

Requires:
Stack S has been created.
Results:
Outputs the elements in S. If S is empty, outputs "Empty stack". This operation is intended for debugging purposes only. It violates the principle of data abstraction by assuming that stack elements can be output using a WRITE statement.

LABORATORY 4: Cover Sheet

Date .... Section ....

Name ....

Place a check mark in the "Assigned" column next to the exercises your instructor has assigned to your class. Attach this cover sheet to the front of the packet of materials you submit following the laboratory.

	Assigned	*Completed*
Prelab Exercise	✓	
In-lab Exercise 1	✓	
In-lab Exercise 2		
In-lab Exercise 3		
In-lab Exercise 4		
Postlab Exercise 1		
Postlab Exercise 2		
		Total

LABORATORY 4: Prelab Exercise

Date .... Section ....

Name ....

In this laboratory, you create two implementations of the Stack ADT. One of these implementations is based on an array, the other is based on a singly linked list.

Step 1: Create a Pascal implementation of the Stack ADT using an array to store the stack elements. Because the stack will change in size, you need to store the array index of the topmost element in the stack (Top), along with the stack elements themselves (Element). Base your implementation on the following TYPE declaration.

```
Stack = RECORD
        Top     : 0..MaxStackArraySize;
        Element : ARRAY [1..MaxStackArraySize] OF StackElement;
     END;
```

Note that a CONST declaration defining MaxStackArraySize and a TYPE declaration defining StackElement must appear in any program that uses this implementation of the Stack ADT.

An array implementation of the StackShowStructure operation is given in the file SHOW4.PAS.

Step 2: Create a file called STACKARR.DEC that contains the TYPE declaration given above and a file called STACKARR.PAS that contains the routines in your implementation. Include comments that describe the array representation of a stack and the operations in your implementation.

Step 3: Create a Pascal implementation of the Stack ADT using a singly linked list to store the stack elements. Each node in the linked list should contain a stack element (Element) and a pointer to the node containing the next element in the stack (Next). Your implementation should maintain a pointer to the node containing the topmost element in the stack (Top). Base your implementation on the following TYPE declarations.

```
StackNodePtr = ^StackNode;

StackNode    = RECORD
                  Element : StackElement;
                  Next    : StackNodePtr;
               END;

Stack        = RECORD
                  Top : StackNodePtr;
               END;
```

Note that you must declare type StackElement in any program that uses the Stack ADT.

A linked list implementation of the StackShowStructure operation is given in the file SHOW4.PAS.

Step 4: Create a file called STACKLNK.DEC that contains the TYPE declarations given above and a file called STACKLNK.PAS that contains the routines in your implementation. Include comments that describe the linked list representation of a stack and the operations in your implementation.

LABORATORY 4: In-lab Exercise 1

Date .... Section ....

Name ....

 The test program in the file TEST4.PAS allows you to interactively test your implementation of the Stack ADT using the following commands.

Command	Action
+x	Push element x on top of the stack.
−	Pop the top element and output it.
E	Report whether the stack is empty.
F	Report whether the stack is full.
C	Clear the stack.
Q	Exit the test program.

Step 1: Complete the following test plan by adding test cases that check whether your implementation of the Stack ADT can do the following: pop an element from a stack that contains only one element, push an element onto a stack that has been emptied by a series of pops, and pop an element from a full stack (if possible). Note that, although expected results are listed for the final command in each command sequence, you should confirm that *every* command produces a correct result. The topmost element in a stack is shown in bold.

Step 2: Use your test plan to check your array implementation of the Stack ADT. If you discover mistakes in this implementation, correct them and execute your test plan again.

Step 3: Modify the test program so that the declarations and routines for your linked list implementation of a stack (STACKLNK.DEC and STACKLNK.PAS) are included in place of those for the array implementation.

Step 4: Use your test plan to check your linked list implementation of the Stack ADT. If you discover mistakes in this implementation, correct them and execute your test plan again.

Test Plan for the operations in the Stack ADT

Test case	Commands	Expected result	Checked
Series of pushes	+a +b +c +d	a b c **d**	
Series of pops	– – –	**a**	
More pushes	+e +f	a e **f**	
More pops	– –	**a**	
Empty? Full?	E F	False False	
Empty the stack	–	Empty stack	
Empty? Full?	E F	True False	

LABORATORY 4: In-lab Exercise 2

Date .... Section ....

Name ....

We say that the arithmetic expression

$$(3+4)*(5/2)$$

is in **infix form** because each operator is placed between its operands. Although we are accustomed to writing arithmetic expressions in this form, infix form has the disadvantage that parentheses must be used to indicate the order in which operators are to be evaluated. These parentheses greatly complicate the process of evaluating an arithmetic expression.

Evaluation is much easier if we can simply evaluate operators from left to right, thereby eliminating the need for parentheses entirely. Unfortunately, this evaluation strategy will not work with the infix form of most arithmetic expressions. However, it *will* work if the expression is in **postfix form**.

In the postfix form of an arithmetic expression, each operator is placed immediately after its operands. The expression given above is expressed in postfix form as

$$34+52/*$$

Expressions in postfix form can be easily evaluated. All you need is a stack to store intermediate results.

Suppose you have an arithmetic expression in postfix form that consists of a sequence of single digit, nonnegative integers, and the four basic arithmetic operators (addition, subtraction, multiplication, and division). This expression can be evaluated using the following algorithm in conjunction with a stack of *real* numbers.

1. Read in the expression character by character. As each character is read in:

   - If the character corresponds to a single digit number (characters '0'..'9'), then push the corresponding real number onto the stack.

   - If the character corresponds to one of the arithmetic operators (characters '+', '−', '*', and '/'), then

     Pop a real number off the stack. Call it Operand1.
     Pop a real number off the stack. Call it Operand2.
     Combine these operands using the arithmetic operator, as follows:

     Result := <Operand2> <Operator> <Operand1>

   - Push Result onto the stack.

2. When the end of the expression is reached, pop the remaining real number off of the stack. This real number is the value of the expression.

Applying this algorithm to the arithmetic expression

$$34+52/*$$

yields the following computation.

'3' : Push 3.0
'4' : Push 4.0
'+' : Pop, Operand1 = 4.0
Pop, Operand2 = 3.0
Combine, Result = 3.0 + 4.0 = 7.0
Push 7.0
'5' : Push 5.0
'2' : Push 2.0
'/' : Pop, Operand1 = 2.0
Pop, Operand2 = 5.0
Combine, Result = 5.0 / 2.0 = 2.5
Push 2.5
'*' : Pop, Operand1 = 2.5
Pop, Operand2 = 7.0
Combine, Result = 7.0 * 2.5 = 17.5
Push 17.5
End : Pop, Value of expression = 17.5

Step 1: Create a Pascal program that reads the postfix form of an arithmetic expression, evaluates it, and outputs the result. Assume that the expression consists of single-digit, nonnegative integers ('0'..'9') and the four basic arithmetic operators ('+', '−', '*' and '/'). Further assume that the arithmetic expression is input from the keyboard with all the characters on one line.

Step 2: Complete the following test plan by filling in the expected result for each arithmetic expression. You may wish to include additional arithmetic expressions in this test plan.

Step 3 Execute this test plan. If you discover mistakes in your program, correct them and execute the test plan again.

Test Plan for the postfix arithmetic expression evaluation program			
Test case	*Arithmetic expression*	*Expected result*	*Checked*
One operator	34+		
Nested operators	34+52/*		
Uneven nesting	93*2+1−		
All operators at end	4675−+*		
Zero dividend	02/		
Single-digit number	7		

LABORATORY 4: In-lab Exercise 3

Date .... Section ....

Name ....

Rather than have the array implementation of a stack grow upward from array entry 1 toward array entry MaxStackArraySize, you can just as easily construct an implementation that begins at array entry MaxStackArraySize and grows downward toward array entry 1. You can combine this "downward" array implementation with the "upward" array implementation you created in the Prelab to form an implementation of a Double Stack ADT in which a pair of stacks occupy the same array—assuming that the total number of elements in *both* stacks never exceeds MaxStackArraySize.

Step 1:   Create an implementation of the Stack ADT using an array in which the stack grows downward. A compatible implementation of the StackShowStructure operation is given in the file SHOW4.PAS.

Step 2:   Create a file called STACKDWN.DEC that contains the TYPE declaration for your "downward" array implementation and a file called STACKDWN.PAS that contains the routines in your implementation.

Step 3:   Modify the test program in the file TEST4.PAS so that the declarations and routines for this implementation (STACKDWN.DEC and STACKDWN.PAS) are included in place of those for the (standard) array implementation.

Step 4:   Use the test plan that you created in In-lab Exercise 1 to check your "downward" array implementation of the Stack ADT. If you discover mistakes in your implementation, correct them and execute your test plan again.

LABORATORY 4: In-lab Exercise 4

Date ....   Section ....

Name ....

At first glance, creating a copy of a stack might seem a simple matter of popping elements off the stack and pushing them onto the copy. Unfortunately, not only does this destroy the contents of the original stack, but the order of the elements in the copy is the reverse of their order in the original stack. Thus, a StackCopy operation makes a valuable addition to your implementation of the Stack ADT.

```
PROCEDURE StackCopy ( S : Stack;
                      VAR CopyS : Stack )
```

Requires:
Stack S has been created.
Results:
Stack CopyS returns a copy of stack S.

Step 1: Create a Pascal implementation of this operation using the linked list representation of a stack.

Step 2: Add your implementation of this operation to the file STACKLNK.PAS.

 Step 3: Add the following code to the test program in the file TEST4.PAS.

```
ELSE IF Cmd = '='
    THEN BEGIN
            WRITELN('Copy stack');
            StackCopy(TestStack,CopyOfStack);
            WRITE('Original stack : ');
            StackShowStructure(TestStack);
            WRITE('Copy of stack  : ');
            StackShowStructure(CopyOfStack);
            WRITELN('Clear original stack');
            StackClear(TestStack);
            WRITE('Original stack : ');
            StackShowStructure(TestStack);
            WRITE('Copy of stack  : ');
            StackShowStructure(CopyOfStack);
            WRITELN;
            END
```

The variable CopyOfStack is of type Stack. Note that this test code clears the original stack in order to establish that your implementation has actually created a new stack and is *not* simply pointing to the original stack.

Step 4: Modify the test program so that the declarations and routines for your linked list implementation of a stack (STACKLNK.DEC and STACKLNK.PAS) are included in place of those for the array implementation.

Step 5: Prepare a test plan for the StackCopy operation that covers stacks of various lengths, including an empty stack.

Step 6: Execute your test plan. If you discover mistakes in your implementation of the StackCopy operation, correct them and execute your test plan again.

Test Plan for the StackCopy operation			
Test case	*Commands*	*Expected result*	*Checked*

LABORATORY 4: Postlab Exercise 1

Date .... Section ....

Name ....

Given the input string 'abc', which permutations of this string can be output by a code fragment consisting of only the statement pairs

```
READ(Ch); Push(S,Ch);    and    Pop(S,Ch); WRITE(Ch);
```

where Ch is a character and S is a stack of characters? Note that each of the statement pairs may be repeated several times within the code fragment and that the statement pairs may be in any order. For instance, the code fragment

```
READ(Ch);    Push(S,Ch);
READ(Ch);    Push(S,Ch);
READ(Ch);    Push(S,Ch);
Pop(S,Ch);   WRITE(Ch);
Pop(S,Ch);   WRITE(Ch);
Pop(S,Ch);   WRITE(Ch);
```

outputs the string 'cba'.

PART A

For each of the permutations listed below, give a code fragment that outputs the permutation *or* a brief explanation of why the permutation cannot be produced.

'abc'	'acb'

'bac'	'bca'
'cab'	'cba'

PART B

Given the input string 'abcd', which permutations beginning with the character 'd' can be output by a code fragment of the form described above? Why can only these permutations be produced?

LABORATORY 4: Postlab Exercise 2

Date .... Section ....

Name ....

In In-Lab Exercise 2, you used a stack to evaluate arithmetic expressions. Describe another application where you might use the Stack ADT. What type of information does your application store in each stack element?

Queue ADT

OVERVIEW

In this laboratory, we examine another constrained linear data structure, the queue. A **queue** is a linear data structure in which the elements are ordered from least recently added to most recently added. Only the least recently added queue element may be referenced directly, and examining this element entails removing it from the queue.

The movement of elements through a queue reflects the "first in, first out" behavior that is characteristic of the flow of customers in a line or the transmission of information across a data channel. Thus, queues are commonly used to regulate—and to model—the movement of physical objects or data through various systems.

QUEUE ADT

ELEMENTS
The elements in a queue are of generic type QueueElement.

STRUCTURE
The queue elements are ordered linearly from least recently added (the front) to most recently added (the rear). Elements are inserted at the rear of the queue (enqueued) and are removed from the front of the queue (dequeued).

OPERATIONS

PROCEDURE QueueCreate (VAR Q : Queue)

Requires:
None.
Results:
Creates an empty queue Q.

```
PROCEDURE Enqueue ( VAR Q : Queue;
                        NewElement : QueueElement )
```

Requires:
Queue Q is not full.
Results:
Inserts queue element NewElement at the rear of Q.

```
PROCEDURE Dequeue ( VAR Q : Queue;
                        VAR FrontElement : QueueElement )
```

Requires:
Queue Q is not empty.
Results:
Removes the least recently added (front) queue element from Q and returns it in FrontElement.

```
FUNCTION QueueEmpty ( Q : Queue ) : BOOLEAN
```

Requires:
Queue Q has been created.
Results:
If Q is empty, then returns true. Otherwise, returns false.

```
FUNCTION QueueFull ( Q : Queue ) : BOOLEAN
```

Requires:
Queue Q has been created.
Results:
If Q is full, then returns true. Otherwise, returns false.

```
PROCEDURE QueueClear ( VAR Q : Queue )
```

Requires:
Queue Q has been created.
Results:
Deletes all elements in Q.

```
PROCEDURE QueueShowStructure ( Q : Queue )
```

Requires:
Queue Q has been created.
Results:
Outputs the elements in Q. If Q is empty, outputs "Empty queue". This operation is intended for debugging purposes only. It violates the principle of data abstraction by assuming that queue elements can be output using a WRITE statement.

LABORATORY 5: Cover Sheet

Date .... Section ....

Name ....

Place a check mark in the "Assigned" column next to the exercises your instructor has assigned to your class. Attach this cover sheet to the front of the packet of materials you submit following the laboratory.

	Assigned	*Completed*
Prelab Exercise	✓	
In-lab Exercise 1	✓	
In-lab Exercise 2		
In-lab Exercise 3		
In-lab Exercise 4		
Postlab Exercise 1		
Postlab Exercise 2		
		Total

LABORATORY 5: Prelab Exercise

Date .... Section ....

Name ....

In this laboratory, you create two implementations of the Queue ADT. One of these implementations is based on an array, the other is based on a singly linked list.

Step 1: Create a Pascal implementation of the Queue ADT using an array to store the queue elements. Because the queue will move through the array, you need to store the array index of the elements at the front (Front) and rear (Rear) of the queue, along with the queue elements themselves (Element). Base your implementation on the following TYPE declaration.

```
Queue = RECORD
          Front,
          Rear    : 0..MaxQueueArraySize;
          Element : ARRAY [1..MaxQueueArraySize] OF QueueElement;
        END;
```

Note that a CONST declaration defining MaxQueueArraySize and a TYPE declaration defining QueueElement must appear in any program that uses this implementation of the Queue ADT.

An array implementation of the QueueShowStructure operation is given in the file SHOW5.PAS.

Step 2: Create a file called QUEUEARR.DEC that contains the TYPE declaration given above and a file called QUEUEARR.PAS that contains the routines in your implementation. Include comments that describe the array representation of a queue and the operations in your implementation.

Step 3: Create a Pascal implementation of the Queue ADT using a singly linked list to store the queue elements. Each node in the linked list should contain a queue element (Element) and a pointer to the node containing the next element in the queue (Next). Your implementation should maintain pointers to the nodes containing the front (Front) and rear (Rear) elements in the queue. Base your implementation on the following TYPE declarations.

```
QueueNodePtr = ^QueueNode;

QueueNode    = RECORD
                 Element : QueueElement;
                 Next    : QueueNodePtr;
               END;

Queue        = RECORD
                 Front,
                 Rear  : QueueNodePtr;
               END;
```

Note that you must declare type QueueElement in any program that uses the Queue ADT.

A linked list implementation of the QueueShowStructure operation is given in the file SHOW5.PAS.

Step 4: Create a file called QUEUELNK.DEC that contains the TYPE declarations given above and a file called QUEUELNK.PAS that contains the routines in your implementation. Include comments that describe the linked list representation of a queue and the operations in your implementation.

LABORATORY 5: In-lab Exercise 1

Date .... Section ....

Name ....

 The test program in the file TEST5.PAS allows you to interactively test your implementation of the Queue ADT using the following commands.

Command	Action
+x	Enqueue element x.
–	Dequeue the front element and output it.
E	Report whether the queue is empty.
F	Report whether the queue is full.
C	Clear the queue.
Q	Exit the test program.

Step 1: Prepare a test plan for your implementations of the Queue ADT. Your test plan should cover a variety of situations, including cases in which you enqueue an element onto a queue that has been emptied by a series of dequeues, combine enqueues and dequeues so that you "go around the end" of the array (array implementation only), and dequeue an element from a full queue (if possible). A test plan form follows.

Step 2: Use your test plan to check your array implementation of the Queue ADT. If you discover mistakes in this implementation, correct them and execute your test plan again.

Step 3: Modify the test program so that the declarations and routines for your linked list implementation of a queue (QUEUELNK.DEC and QUEUELNK.PAS) are included in place of those for the array implementation.

Step 4: Use your test plan to check your linked list implementation of the Queue ADT. If you discover mistakes in this implementation, correct them and execute your test plan again.

Test Plan for the operations in the Queue ADT			
Test case	*Commands*	*Expected result*	*Checked*

LABORATORY 5: In-lab Exercise 2

Date .... Section ....

Name ....

You can create a model of a line of customers in a store by using a queue in which each element corresponds to an individual customer, and the flow of elements through the queue corresponds to the flow of customers through the line. Suppose you wish to model the flow of customers through a line that has the following properties:

- One customer is served and leaves the line every minute (assuming that there is at least one customer waiting to be served during that minute).

- From zero to two customers arrive and join the line every minute, where there is a 50% chance that no customers arrive, a 25% chance that one customer arrives, and a 25% chance that two customers arrive.

The passage of time can be modeled by a loop in which every pass through the loop corresponds to one minute of "real" time. You can simulate the flow of customers through the line using the following approach.

```
Initialize an integer variable Minute to zero.
Create an empty queue.
        REPEAT
        If the queue is not empty, then remove the first customer.
        Compute a random integer value between 0 and 3.
        CASE random value OF
                0, 1: No customers.
                2   : Add one customer.
                3   : Add two customers.
        END
        Increment Minute.
        UNTIL the specified number of minutes have elapsed.
```

 Step 1: Using the program shell given in the file STOSHELL.PAS as a basis, create a Pascal program that uses the Queue ADT to implement the model described above. Your program should update the following information during each simulated minute, that is, during each pass through the loop.

- The total number of customers served.

- The combined length of time that these customers spent waiting in line.

- The maximum length of time that any of these customers spent waiting in line.

In order to compute how long a customer waited to be served, you need to store the "minute" that the customer was added to the queue as part of the queue element corresponding to that customer.

Step 2: Use your program to simulate the flow of customers through a line and complete the following table.

Time (minutes)	Total number of customers served	Average wait	Longest wait
30			
60			
120			
480			

Note that the average wait is the combined waiting time divided by the total number of customers served.

LABORATORY 5: In-lab Exercise 3

Date .... Section ....

Name ....

A **deque** (double-ended queue) is a linear data structure that allows elements to be inserted and removed at both ends. Adding the operations described below will transform your Queue ADT into a Deque ADT.

```
PROCEDURE QueuePutFront ( VAR Q : Queue;
                          NewElement : QueueElement )
```

Requires:
Queue Q is not full.

Results:
Inserts element NewElement at the front of Q. The order of the pre-existing elements remains unchanged.

```
PROCEDURE QueueGetRear ( VAR Q : Queue;
                         VAR RearElement : QueueElement )
```

Requires:
Queue Q is not empty.

Results:
Removes the least recently added (rear) element from Q and returns it in RearElement. The remainder of the queue is left unchanged.

Step 1: Create Pascal implementations of these operations using the array representation of a queue.

Step 2: Add your implementation of these operations to the file QUEUEARR.PAS.

 Step 3: Add the following code to the test program in the file TEST5.PAS.

```
ELSE IF Cmd = '>'
   THEN BEGIN
        WRITELN('Put in front ',QueueElement);
        QueuePutFront(TestQueue,QueueElement);
        END
ELSE IF Cmd = '='
   THEN BEGIN
        QueueGetRear(TestQueue,QueueElement);
        WRITELN('From rear ',QueueElement);
        END
```

You also must change the statement

```
IF Cmd = '+'
   THEN READLN(TestElement)
   ELSE READLN;
```

to the statement

```
IF ( Cmd = '+' ) OR ( Cmd = '>' )
   THEN READLN(TestElement)
   ELSE READLN;
```

so you can specify the element that is to be inserted at the front of the queue.

Step 4:   Prepare a test plan for these operations that includes test cases that cover inserting an element at the front of a newly emptied queue, removing an element from the rear of a queue containing only one element, and "going around the end" of the array using the QueuePutFront and QueueGetRear operations.

Step 5:   Execute your test plan. If you discover mistakes in your implementation of these operations, correct them and execute your test plan again.

Test Plan for the QueuePutFront and QueueGetRear operations			
Test case	*Commands*	*Expected result*	*Checked*

LABORATORY 5: In-lab Exercise 4

Date .... Section ....

Name ....

When a queue is used as part of a model or simulation, the modeler is often very interested in how many elements are in the queue at various times. This statistic is produced by the following operation.

```
FUNCTION QueueLength ( Q : Queue ) : INTEGER
```

Requires:
Queue Q has been created.
Results:
Returns the number of elements in Q.

Step 1: Create a Pascal implementation of the QueueLength operation using the array representation of a queue.

Step 2: Add your implementation of this operation to the file QUEUEARR.PAS.

 Step 3: Add the following code to the test program in the file TEST5.PAS.

```
ELSE IF Cmd = '#'
    THEN WRITELN('Queue length = ',QueueLength(TestQueue))
```

Step 4: Prepare a test plan for this operation that covers queues of various lengths, including both empty and full queues. A test plan form follows.

Step 5: Execute your test plan. If you discover mistakes in your implementation of the QueueLength operation, correct them and execute your test plan again.

Test Plan for the QueueLength operation			
Test case	*Commands*	*Expected result*	*Checked*

LABORATORY 5: Postlab Exercise 1

Date .... Section ....

Name ....

PART A

Given the following memory requirements

Integer	2 bytes
Address (pointer)	4 bytes

and a queue containing one hundred integers, compare the amount of memory used by your array representation of this queue with the amount of memory used by your singly linked list representation. Assume that the array representation allows a queue to contain a maximum of one hundred elements (that is, MaxQueueArraySize=100).

PART B

Suppose that you have ten queues of integers. Of these ten queues, four are 50% full, and the remaining six are 10% full. Compare the amount of memory used by your array representation of these queues with the amount of memory used by your singly linked list representation. Assume that the array representation allows a queue to contain a maximum of one hundred elements.

LABORATORY 5: Postlab Exercise 2

Date .... Section ....

Name ....

In In-lab Exercise 2, you used a queue to simulate the flow of customers through a line. Describe another application where you might use the Queue ADT. What type of information does your application store in each queue element?

List ADT III

OVERVIEW

When we created a singly linked list implementation of the List ADT in Laboratory 2, we assumed that lists ordinarily would be processed from beginning to end. When you actually use the List ADT in your applications programs, you may discover that this assumption is not accurate and that considerable time is spent going in the opposite direction. In this laboratory, you create an implementation of the List ADT based on a circular doubly linked list. This implementation supports efficient movement through the list in either direction.

LIST ADT

ELEMENTS
The elements in a list are of generic type ListElement.

STRUCTURE
The elements in a list form a linear structure; that is, the list elements follow one after the other, from the beginning of the list (the first element) to the end of the list (the last element). The order of the list elements is determined by when and where each element is inserted and is *not* a function of the data contained in the list elements.

At any point, one element in any nonempty list is designated as the **current list element**. Insertions and deletions are made relative to the current list element. You can travel through the list by changing this designation.

OPERATIONS

PROCEDURE ListCreate (VAR L : List)

Requires:
None.
Results:
Creates an empty list L.

```
PROCEDURE ListInsert ( VAR L : List )
                           NewElement : ListElement )
```

Requires:
List L is not full.
Results:
Inserts list element NewElement into L. If L is not empty, then NewElement is inserted immediately after the current list element. Otherwise, NewElement is inserted as the first (and only) element in L. In either case, NewElement becomes the current list element.

```
PROCEDURE ListDelete ( VAR L : List )
```

Requires:
List L is not empty.
Results:
Deletes the current list element from L. If the resulting list is not empty, then the element that followed the deleted element becomes the current list element. If the deleted element was at the end of the list, then the first element in the list becomes the current list element.

```
PROCEDURE ListCurrent ( L : List;
                           VAR CurrentElement : ListElement )
```

Requires:
List L is not empty.
Results:
CurrentElement returns a copy of the current list element.

```
PROCEDURE ListReplace ( VAR L : List;
                           NewElement : ListElement )
```

Requires:
List L is not empty.
Results:
Replaces the current list element with list element NewElement.

```
PROCEDURE ListGotoNext ( VAR L : List )
```

Requires:
List L is not empty, and the current list element is not at the end of L.
Results:
The element immediately after the current list element becomes the current list element.

```
PROCEDURE ListGotoPrior ( VAR L : List )
```

Requires:
List L is not empty, and the current list element is not at the beginning of L.
Results:
The element immediately before the current list element becomes the current list element.

```
PROCEDURE ListGotoBeginning ( VAR L : List )
```

Requires:
List L is not empty.
Results:
The element at the beginning of L becomes the current list element.

PROCEDURE ListGotoEnd (VAR L : List)

Requires:
List L is not empty.

Results:
The element at the end of L becomes the current list element.

FUNCTION ListEmpty (L : List) : BOOLEAN

Requires:
List L has been created.

Results:
If L is empty, then returns true. Otherwise, returns false.

FUNCTION ListFull (L : List) : BOOLEAN

Requires:
List L has been created.

Results:
If L is full, then returns true. Otherwise, returns false.

FUNCTION ListAtBeginning (L : List) : BOOLEAN

Requires:
List L is not empty.

Results:
If the current list element is at the beginning of L, then returns true. Otherwise, returns false.

FUNCTION ListAtEnd (L : List) : BOOLEAN

Requires:
List L is not empty.

Results:
If the current list element is at the end of L, then returns true. Otherwise, returns false.

PROCEDURE ListClear (VAR L : List)

Requires:
List L has been created.

Results:
Deletes all elements in L.

PROCEDURE ListShowStructure (L : List)

Requires:
List L has been created.

Results:
Outputs the elements in L. If L is empty, outputs "Empty list". This operation is intended for debugging purposes only. It violates the principle of data abstraction by assuming that list elements can be output using a WRITE statement.

LABORATORY 6: Cover Sheet

Date .... Section ....

Name ....

Place a check mark in the "Assigned" column next to the exercises your instructor has assigned to your class. Attach this cover sheet to the front of the packet of materials you submit following the laboratory.

	Assigned	*Completed*
Prelab Exercise	✓	
In-lab Exercise 1	✓	
In-lab Exercise 2		
In-lab Exercise 3		
In-lab Exercise 4		
Postlab Exercise 1		
Postlab Exercise 2		
		Total

LABORATORY 6: Prelab Exercise

Date .... Section ....

Name ....

In a doubly linked list, each node N contains a pair of pointers. One pointer points to the node that precedes N, and the other pointer points to the node that follows N. As a result, traveling backward toward the beginning of the list is just as efficient as traveling forward toward the end.

Step 1:   Create a Pascal implementation of the List ADT using a circular doubly linked list to store the list elements. Each node in the linked list should contain a list element (Element), a pointer to the node containing the next element in the list (Next), and a pointer to the node containing the previous element in the list (Prior). Your implementation should maintain pointers to the first node in the list (Head) and the node containing the current list element (Current). Base your implementation on the following TYPE declarations.

```
ListNodePtr  =  ^ListNode;

ListNode     =  RECORD
                   Element : ListElement;
                   Prior,
                   Next    : ListNodePtr;
                END;

List         =  RECORD
                   Head,
                   Current : ListNodePtr;
                END;
```

Note that you must declare type ListElement in any program that uses the List ADT.
An implementation of the ListShowStructure operation is given in the file SHOW6.PAS.

Step 2:   Create a file called LISTDBL.DEC that contains the TYPE declarations given above and a file called LISTDBL.PAS that contains the routines in your implementation. Include comments that describe the circular doubly linked list representation of a list and the operations in your implementation.

LABORATORY 6: In-lab Exercise 1

Date .... Section ....

Name ....

 The test program in the file TEST6.PAS allows you to interactively test your implementation of the List ADT using the following commands.

Command	Action
+x	Insert element x.
–	Delete the current list element.
@	Get the current list element and output it.
=x	Replace the current list element with element x.
N	Go to the next list element.
P	Go to the prior list element.
<	Go to the beginning of the list.
>	Go to the end of the list.
E	Report whether the list is empty.
F	Report whether the list is full.
[	Report whether the current list element is at the beginning of the list.
]	Report whether the current list element is at the end of the list.
C	Clear the list.
Q	Quit the test program.

Step 1: Prepare a test plan for your implementation of the List ADT. Your test plan should cover the application of each operation to elements at the beginning, middle, and end of lists (where appropriate).

Step 2: Execute your test plan. If you discover mistakes in your implementation of the List ADT, correct them and execute your test plan again.

Test Plan for the operations in the List ADT			
Test case	*Commands*	*Expected result*	*Checked*

LABORATORY 6: In-lab Exercise 2

Date .... Section ....

Name ....

A slide show consists of a sequence of slides. Rather than simply displaying the slides in order from beginning to end, most presentation systems allow a user to move forward or backward at any point during the presentation. The resulting slide show presentation process is outlined below.

```
Read the slides in the show from a data file.
Go to the first slide in the show.
    REPEAT
    Clear the screen (either directly, or by scrolling until the last slide has moved off
        the top of the screen).
    Display the current slide, followed by the prompt 'Command:'.
    Read a command from the user.
    CASE command OF
        'N': Go to the next slide (if possible).
        'P': Go to the previous slide (if possible).
    END
    UNTIL the command 'Q' is input.
```

Step 1:   Create a Pascal program that implements this slide show presentation process using the operations in the List ADT. Assume each slide is a 10x35 array of characters. Base your program on the following TYPE declarations.

```
Slide        =  ARRAY [ 1..10, 1..35 ] OF CHAR;
ListElement  =  Slide;
```

Note that these declarations produce a list element that is a two-dimensional array, rather than one of Pascal's native data types (INTEGER, CHAR, and so on). List elements of this type should not cause problems with the routines in your implementation of the List ADT, with the exception of the ListShowStructure operation. Inactivate this operation by commenting out the ListShowStructure procedure.

Step 2:   Test your program using the slide show in the data file SLIDESHW.DAT. Each line in this file corresponds to one row in a slide, with every ten lines forming a complete slide.

LABORATORY 6: In-lab Exercise 3

Date .... Section ....

Name ....

A list can be reversed by either relinking the nodes in the list into a new (reversed) order, or leaving the node structure intact and exchanging elements between pairs of nodes. Use one of these strategies to implement the following operation.

PROCEDURE ListReverse (VAR L : List)

Requires:
List L has been created.
Results:
Reverses the order of the elements in L. The current list element designation remains unchanged.

Step 1: Create a Pascal implementation of this operation.

Step 2: Add your implementation of this operation to the file LISTDBL.PAS.

Step 3: Add the following code to the test program in the file TEST6.PAS.

```
ELSE IF ( Cmd = 'R' ) OR ( Cmd = 'r' )
   THEN BEGIN
        WRITELN('Reverse list');
        ListReverse(TestList);
        END
```

Step 4: Prepare a test plan for the ListReverse operation that covers lists of various lengths, including lists that contain a single element. A test plan form follows.

Step 5: Execute your test plan. If you discover mistakes in your implementation of the ListReverse operation, correct them and execute your test plan again.

Test Plan for the ListReverse operation			
Test case	*Commands*	*Expected result*	*Checked*

LABORATORY 6: In-lab Exercise 4

Date .... Section ....

Name ....

In many applications, you need to know both the size of the list and the relative position of the current list element.

Step 1: Modify the routines in your circular doubly linked list implementation of the List ADT so the following list attributes are constantly maintained.

> Size : The number of elements in the list.
> Pos : The numeric position of the current list element, where the first element in the list occupies position 1, the second element occupies position 2, and so forth.

For example, when the current list element is the fifth element in a list of twenty, Size is twenty and Pos is five. Base your modifications on the following TYPE declarations.

```
ListNodePtr  =  ^ListNode;
ListNode     =  RECORD
                    Element : ListElement;
                    Prior,
                    Next    : ListNodePtr;
                END;

List         =  RECORD
                    Size,
                    Pos     : INTEGER;
                    Head,
                    Current : ListNodePtr;
                END;
```

Step 2: Create a file called LISTDBL2.DEC that contains these TYPE declarations and a file called LISTDBL2.PAS that contains the routines in your modified implementation of the List ADT.

Step 3: If you are to reference the Size and Pos attributes within applications programs, you must have List ADT operations that return these attributes. Create Pascal implementations of the following operations.

FUNCTION ListSize (L : List) : INTEGER

Requires:
List L has been created.
Results:
Returns the number of elements in L.

```
FUNCTION ListPosition ( L : List ) : INTEGER
```

Requires:
List L is not empty.
Results:
Returns the numeric position of the current list element in L.

Step 4:   Add your implementation of these operations to the (modified) routines in the file LISTDBL2.PAS.

Step 5:   Add the following code to the test program in the file TEST6.PAS.

```
IF ListSize(TestList) <> 0
   THEN WRITE('Position ',ListPosition(TestList),'  ');
WRITELN('Size ',ListSize(TestList));
```

Step 6:   Modify the test program so the declarations and routines that incorporate your changes (LISTDBL2.DEC and LISTDBL2.PAS) are included in place of the ones you created in the Prelab.

Step 7:   Prepare a test plan for these operations that checks the size of various lists (including the empty list) and the numeric position of elements at the beginning, middle, and end of lists.

Step 8:   Execute your test plan. If you discover mistakes in your implementation of these operations, correct them and execute your test plan again.

Test Plan for the ListSize and ListPosition operations			
Test case	*Commands*	*Expected result*	*Checked*

LABORATORY 6: Postlab Exercise 1

Date .... Section ....

Name ....

PART A

Given a list containing N elements, develop worst-case, order-of-magnitude estimates of the execution time of the following List ADT operations, assuming they are implemented using a circular doubly linked list. Briefly explain your reasoning behind each estimate.

ListInsert   O(   )

Explanation:

ListDelete   O(   )

Explanation:

ListGotoNext   O(   )

Explanation:

ListGotoPrior   O(   )

Explanation:

PART B

Would these estimates be the same for an implementation of the List ADT based on a noncircular doubly linked list? Explain why or why not.

LABORATORY 6: Postlab Exercise 2

Date .... Section ....

Name ....

PART A

Given the following memory requirements

Character	1 byte
Integer	2 bytes
Address (pointer)	4 bytes

and a list containing N integers, compare the amount of memory used by your singly linked list representation of the list with the amount of memory used by your circular doubly linked list representation.

PART B

Suppose the list contains N elements of type Slide (In-Lab Exercise 2). Compare the amount of memory used by your singly linked list representation of the list with the amount of memory used by your circular doubly linked representation.

Ordered List ADT

OVERVIEW

In an **ordered list** the elements are maintained in ascending or descending order based on the data contained in the list elements. Typically, the contents of one field are used to determine the ordering. This field is referred to as the **key field**, or **key**.

In this laboratory, we assume that each element in an ordered list has a key that uniquely identifies the element. No two elements in any ordered list have the same key. As a result, you can use an element's key to efficiently retrieve the element from an ordered list. How you search for the key depends on how the ordered list is represented. This laboratory focuses on two implementations of the Ordered List ADT. One implementation uses an array to store the list elements, and a binary search to locate elements. The other uses a linked list in conjunction with a sequential search.

ORDERED LIST ADT

ELEMENTS

Each element in an ordered list has a key that uniquely identifies it. Elements usually include additional data.

STRUCTURE

The list elements are stored in ascending order based on their keys. For each list element E, the element that precedes E has a key that is less than E's key, and the element that follows E has a key that is greater than E's key.

At any point, one element in any nonempty list is designated as the **current list element**. You can travel through the list by changing this designation.

OPERATIONS

PROCEDURE OrdListCreate (VAR L : OrdList)

Requires:
None.
Results:
Creates an empty list L.

```
PROCEDURE OrdListInsert ( VAR L : OrdList;
                             NewElement : OrdListElement )
```

Requires:
List L is not full.

Results:
Inserts list element NewElement in its appropriate position within list L. If an element with the same key as NewElement already exists in L, then updates that element's nonkey fields with NewElement's nonkey fields. The inserted (or updated) element becomes the current list element.

```
FUNCTION OrdListRetrieve ( VAR L : OrdList;
                              SrchKey : OrdListKey;
                              VAR SrchElement : OrdListElement ): BOOLEAN
```

Requires:
Ordered list L has been created.

Results:
Searches L for the element with key SrchKey. If this element is found, then returns true with SrchElement returning the element. Otherwise, returns false with SrchElement undefined. In addition, if the element is found, then it becomes the current list element. Otherwise, the current list element designation remains unchanged.

```
PROCEDURE OrdListDelete ( VAR L : OrdList )
```

Requires:
List L is not empty.

Results:
Deletes the current list element from L. If the resulting list is not empty, then the element that followed the deleted element becomes the current list element. If the deleted element was at the end of the list, then the first element in the list becomes the current list element.

```
PROCEDURE OrdListCurrent ( L : OrdList;
                              VAR CurrentElement : OrdListElement )
```

Requires:
List L is not empty.

Results:
CurrentElement returns a copy of the current list element.

```
PROCEDURE OrdListReplace ( VAR L : OrdList;
                              NewElement : OrdListElement )
```

Requires:
List L is not empty.

Results:
Replaces the current list element with list element NewElement. Note that this entails deleting the current list element and inserting NewElement. The (inserted) replacement becomes the current list element.

PROCEDURE OrdListGotoNext (VAR L : OrdList)

Requires:
List L is not empty, and the current list element is not at the end of L.
Results:
The element immediately after the current list element becomes the current list element.

PROCEDURE OrdListGotoPrior (VAR L : OrdList)

Requires:
List L is not empty, and the current list element is not at the beginning of L.
Results:
The element immediately before the current list element becomes the current list element.

PROCEDURE OrdListGotoBeginning (VAR L : OrdList)

Requires:
List L is not empty.
Results:
The element at the beginning of L becomes the current list element.

PROCEDURE OrdListGotoEnd (VAR L : OrdList)

Requires:
List L is not empty.
Results:
The element at the end of L becomes the current list element.

FUNCTION OrdListEmpty (L : OrdList) : BOOLEAN

Requires:
List L has been created.
Results:
If L is empty, then returns true. Otherwise, returns false.

FUNCTION OrdListFull (L : OrdList) : BOOLEAN

Requires:
List L has been created.
Results:
If L is full, then returns true. Otherwise, returns false.

FUNCTION OrdListAtBeginning (L : OrdList) : BOOLEAN

Requires:
List L is not empty.
Results:
If the current list element is at the beginning of L, then returns true. Otherwise, returns false.

FUNCTION OrdListAtEnd (L : OrdList) : BOOLEAN

Requires:
List L is not empty.
Results:
If the current list element is at the end of L, then returns true. Otherwise, returns false.

PROCEDURE OrdListClear (VAR L : OrdList)

Requires:
List L has been created.
Results:
Deletes all elements in L.

PROCEDURE OrdListShowStructure (L : OrdList)

Requires:
List L has been created.
Results:
Outputs the keys of the elements in L. If L is empty, outputs "Empty list". This operation is intended for debugging purposes only. It violates the principle of data abstraction by assuming that keys can be output using a WRITE statement.

LABORATORY 7: Cover Sheet

Date .... Section ....

Name ....

Place a check mark in the "Assigned" column next to the exercises your instructor has assigned to your class. Attach this cover sheet to the front of the packet of materials you submit following the laboratory.

	Assigned	*Completed*
Prelab Exercise	✓	
In-lab Exercise 1	✓	
In-lab Exercise 2		
In-lab Exercise 3		
In-lab Exercise 4		
Postlab Exercise 1		
Postlab Exercise 2		
		Total

Date .... Section ....

Name ....

This exercise uses the array and linked list implementations of the List ADT you created in Laboratories 2 and 3 as the basis for the development of array and linked list implementations of the Ordered List ADT.

Step 1: Modify the array implementation of the List ADT you developed in Laboratory 2 to form an array implementation of the Ordered List ADT. Each element in the array should have a unique key (Element[ ].Key). Base your implementation on the following TYPE declaration.

```
OrdList = RECORD
              Size,
              Current : 0..MaxOrdListArraySize;
              Element : ARRAY [ 1..MaxOrdListArraySize ] OF
                                               OrdListElement;
          END;
```

Note that a CONST declaration defining MaxOrdListArraySize and TYPE declarations of the following form must appear in any program that uses this implementation of the Ordered List ADT.

```
OrdListKey     = ...
OrdListElement = RECORD
                     Key   : OrdListKey;
                     ...
                 END;
```

Assume that OrdListKey is a type that can be compared using the standard comparison operators ('<', '=', etc.).

Your implementation of the OrdListRetrieve operation should use a binary search to determine where an element is located. Similarly, your implementation of the OrdListInsert operation should use a binary search to determine where to insert a new element.

An array implementation of the OrdListShowStructure operation is given in the file SHOW7.PAS.

Step 2: Create a file called ORDERARR.DEC that contains the TYPE declaration for type OrdList and a file called ORDERARR.PAS that contains the routines in your implementation. Include comments that describe the array representation of an ordered list and the operations in your implementation.

Step 3: Modify the linked list implementation of the List ADT you developed in Laboratory 3 to form a linked list implementation of the Ordered List ADT. Each element in the list should have a unique key (Element.Key). Base your implementation on the following TYPE declarations.

```
OrdListNodePtr = ^OrdListNode;

OrdListNode    = RECORD
                     Element : OrdListElement;
                     Next    : OrdListNodePtr;
                 END;

OrdList        = RECORD
                     Head,
                     Current : OrdListNodePtr;
                 END;
```

Note that TYPE declarations defining OrdListKey and OrdListElement must appear in any program that uses this implementation of the Ordered List ADT.

A linked list implementation of the OrdListShowStructure operation is given in the file SHOW 7.PAS.

Step 4: Create a file called ORDERLNK.DEC that contains the OrdListNodePtr, OrdListNode, and OrdList TYPE declarations, and a file called ORDERLNK.PAS that contains the routines in your implementation. Include comments that describe the linked list representation of an ordered list and the operations in your implementation.

LABORATORY 7: In-lab Exercise 1

Date .... Section ....

Name ....

 The test program in the file TEST7.PAS allows you to interactively test an implementation of the Ordered List ADT using the following commands.

Command	Action
+key	Insert (or update) the element with the specified key.
?key	Retrieve the element with the specified key and output it.
–	Delete the current list element.
@	Get the current list element and output it.
=key	Replace the current list element with the element with the specified key.
N	Go to the next list element.
P	Go to the prior list element.
<	Go to the beginning of the list.
>	Go to the end of the list.
E	Report whether the list is empty.
F	Report whether the list is full.
[	Report whether the current list element is at the beginning of the list.
]	Report whether the current list element is at the end of the list.
C	Clear the list.
Q	Quit the test program.

Step 1:   Prepare a test plan for your implementations of the Ordered List ADT. Your test plan should cover the application of each operation to elements at the beginning, middle, and end of lists (where appropriate). A test plan form follows.

Step 2:   Use your test plan to check your array implementation of the Ordered List ADT. If you discover mistakes in this implementation, correct them and execute your test plan again.

Step 3: Modify the test program so the declarations and routines for your linked list implementation of an ordered list (ORDERLNK.DEC and ORDERLNK.PAS) are included in place of those for the array implementation.

Step 4: Use your test plan to check your linked list implementation of the Ordered List ADT. If you discover mistakes in this implementation, correct them and execute your test plan again.

Test Plan for the operations in the Ordered List ADT			
Test case	Commands	Expected result	Checked

LABORATORY 7: In-lab Exercise 2

Date .... Section ....

Name ....

When a communications site transmits a message through a packet-switching network, it does not send the message as a continuous stream of data. Instead, it divides the message into pieces called **packets**. These packets are sent through the network to the receiving site, which reassembles the message. Packets may be transmitted through the network to the receiving site along different paths. As a result, they are likely to arrive out of sequence. In order for the receiving site to reassemble the message correctly, each packet must include not only a piece of the message, but also the relative position of that packet within the message.

For example, if we break 'A SHORT MESSAGE' into packets five characters long and preface each packet with a number denoting its position in the message, the result is the following three packets.

```
1 A SHO
2 RT ME
3 SSAGE
```

No matter what order these packets arrive in, the receiving site can correctly reassemble the message by placing the packets in ascending order based on the packet numbers.

Step 1: Create a Pascal program that reassembles the packets contained in a text file and outputs the corresponding message. Your program should use the Ordered List ADT to assist in reassembling the packets in a message. Assume that each packet in the message file contains a packet number and five characters from the message (the packet format shown above). Base your program on the following TYPE declarations.

```
CONST PacketSize = 5;   {  # characters in a packet  }

TYPE OrdListKey     = INTEGER;      {  Packet number  }
     PacketContents = RECORD
                        Key  : OrdListKey;
                        Body : ARRAY [ 1..PacketSize ] OF CHAR;
                      END;
     OrdListElement = PacketContents;
```

Step 2: Test your program using the message in the text file MESSAGE.DAT.

LABORATORY 7: In-lab Exercise 3

Date .... Section ....

Name ....

Suppose you wish to combine the elements in two ordered lists of similar size. You could use repeated calls to the OrdListInsert operation to insert the elements from one list into the other, but the resulting process would not be efficient. A more effective approach is to use a specialized **merge** operation that takes advantage of the fact that the lists are ordered.

```
PROCEDURE OrdListMerge ( VAR L : OrdList;
                             FromL : OrdList  )
```

Requires:
Ordered lists FromL and L have no elements with the same key.
Results:
Merges the elements in FromL into L. List FromL is unchanged.

Step 1: Create a Pascal implementation of this operation using the array representation of an ordered list. Note that even before you start to merge the lists, you already know how much larger list L will grow (remember, no key is in both lists). By traversing FromL and L in parallel, starting with their highest keys and working backward, you can perform the merge in a single pass through the lists.

Step 2: Add your implementation of this operation to the file ORDERARR.PAS.

 Step 3: Add the following code to the test program in the file TEST7TWO.PAS.

```
OrdListMerge(TestList1,TestList2);
WRITELN;
WRITELN('List 1 :');
OrdListShowStructure(TestList1);
```

Step 4: Prepare a test plan for the OrdListMerge operation that covers lists of various lengths, including empty lists and lists that combine to produce a full list. A test plan form follows.

Step 5: Execute your test plan. If you discover mistakes in your implementation of the OrdListMerge operation, correct them and execute your test plan again.

Test Plan for the OrdListMerge operation			
Test case	*Lists*	*Expected result*	*Checked*

LABORATORY 7: In-lab Exercise 4

Date .... Section ....

Name ....

A set of objects can be represented in many ways. If you use an *unordered* linked list to represent a set, then performing set operations such as intersection, union, difference, and subset require up to $O(N^2)$ time. By using an ordered linked list to represent a set, however, you can reduce the execution time for these set operations to $O(N)$, a substantial improvement. Consider the subset operation described below.

FUNCTION OrdListSubset (L, SubL : OrdList) : BOOLEAN

Requires:
The elements in ordered lists SubL and L have only key fields.
Results:
Returns true if every key in SubL is also in L. Otherwise, returns false.

If lists L and SubL are stored as unordered linked lists, this operation requires you to traverse L once for *each* element in SubL. But, if the lists are stored as ordered linked lists, only a single traversal is required. The key is to move through the lists in parallel.

Step 1:   Create a Pascal implementation of this operation using the linked list representation of an ordered list.

Step 2:   Add your implementation of this operation to the file ORDERLNK.PAS.

Step 3:   Add the following code to the test program in the file TEST7TWO.PAS.

```
WRITELN;
IF OrdListSubset(TestList1,TestList2)
   THEN WRITELN('List 2 is a subset of list 1')
   ELSE WRITELN('List 2 is NOT a subset of list 1');
```

Step 4:   Modify the test program so the declarations and routines for your linked list implementation of an ordered list (ORDERLNK.DEC and ORDERLNK.PAS) are included in place of those for the array implementation.

Step 5:   Prepare a test plan for the OrdListSubset operation that covers lists of various lengths, including empty lists. Note that an empty list is a subset of every list. A test plan form follows.

Step 6:   Execute your test plan. If you discover mistakes in your implementation of the OrdListSubset operation, correct them and execute your test plan again.

Test Plan for the OrdListSubset operation			
Test case	*Lists*	*Expected result*	*Checked*

LABORATORY 7: Postlab Exercise 1

Date .... Section ....

Name ....

PART A

Given an ordered list containing N elements, develop worst-case, order-of-magnitude estimates of the execution time of the steps in the OrdListInsert operation, assuming that it is implemented using an array in conjunction with a binary search. Briefly explain your reasoning behind each estimate.

Array implementation of the OrdListInsert operation	
Find the insertion point	O( )
Insert element	O( )
Entire operation	O( )
Explanation:	

PART B

Given an ordered list containing N elements, develop worst-case, order-of-magnitude estimates of the execution time of the steps in the OrdListInsert operation, assuming that it is implemented using a singly linked list. Briefly explain your reasoning behind each estimate.

Linked list implementation of the OrdListInsert operation	
Find the insertion point	O( )
Insert element	O( )
Entire operation	O( )
Explanation:	

PART B

LABORATORY 7: Postlab Exercise 2

Date .... Section ....

Name ....

Describe an application of the Ordered List ADT that your array implementation would perform better than your linked list implementation. How does your application emphasize the strengths of the array implementation?

Recursion with Linked Lists

OVERVIEW

Recursion is a potent tool in any programmer's repertoire. In this laboratory, you examine how recursion can be used to manipulate linked lists—in particular,

- how you can use recursion to implement a traversal of a singly linked list that starts at the end of the list and progresses back to the beginning, and

- how you can use recursion to reorganize a singly linked list (adding, deleting, or moving elements) by passing pointer variables using call-by-reference.

The latter concept is especially important. The restructuring techniques you develop in this laboratory provide the framework on which you will build your implementations of hierarchical data structures in later laboratories.

LABORATORY 8: Cover Sheet

Date .... Section ....

Name ....

Place a check mark in the "Assigned" column next to the exercises your instructor has assigned to your class. Attach this cover sheet to the front of the packet of materials you submit following the laboratory.

	Assigned	*Completed*
Prelab Exercise	✓	
In-lab Exercise 1	✓	
In-lab Exercise 2		
In-lab Exercise 3		
In-lab Exercise 4		
Postlab Exercise 1		
Postlab Exercise 2		
		Total

LABORATORY 8: Prelab Exercise

Date .... Section ....

Name ....

 We begin by examining a set of recursive routines that perform known functions. These routines are collected in the file RECLIST.PAS. You can execute them using the test program in the file TEST8.PAS. Note that this test program requires the ListCreate, ListInsert, and ListShowStructure operations you created in Laboratory 3.

PART A

One of the most common reasons for applying recursion to singly linked lists is to support traversal of the list from the last element back to the first, as in the ListWriteMirror procedure given below.

```
PROCEDURE ListWriteMirror ( L : List );

{  Outputs the elements in list L from first to last, and then  }
{  last to first. Assumes that objects of type ListElement can  }
{  be output using a WRITE statement.                           }

    PROCEDURE WriteMirrorNode ( P : ListNodePtr );
    BEGIN
    IF P <> NIL
        THEN BEGIN
            WRITE(P^.Element);
            WriteMirrorNode(P^.Next);
            WRITE(P^.Element);
            END;
    END;

BEGIN
WRITE('Mirror : ');
WriteMirrorNode(L.Head);
WRITELN;
END;
```

Step 1:   Add the following statement to the test program in the file TEST8.PAS.

```
ListWriteMirror(TestList);
```

Step 2:   Execute the ListWriteMirror procedure using the following list.

```
TestList.Head → 'A' → 'B' → 'C' → NIL
```

Step 3:   Describe what each statement in procedure WriteMirrorNode does during the call in which parameter P points to the node containing 'A'.

Step 4:   What is the significance of the call to procedure WriteMirrorNode in which parameter P is NIL?

Step 5:   Describe how the calls to procedure WriteMirrorNode combine to produce the "mirrored" output. Draw a diagram to illustrate your answer.

PART B

This same "last to first" traversal plays an important role in the ListReverse procedure given below.

```
PROCEDURE ListReverse ( VAR L : List );

{  Reverses the order of the elements in list L.  }

    PROCEDURE ReverseNode ( P, NextP : ListNodePtr;
                            VAR HeadP : ListNodePtr );
    BEGIN
    IF NextP <> NIL
       THEN BEGIN
            ReverseNode(NextP,NextP^.Next,HeadP);
            NextP^.Next := P;
            END
       ELSE HeadP := P;
    END;

BEGIN
ReverseNode(NIL,L.Head,L.Head);
END;
```

Step 1: Add the following statement to the test program in the file TEST8.PAS.

```
ListReverse(TestList);
```

Step 2: Execute the ListReverse procedure using the following list.

```
TestList.Head → 'A' → 'B' → 'C' → NIL
```

Step 3: Describe what each statement in procedure ReverseNode does during the call in which parameter P points to the node containing 'B'. In particular, how are the links to and from this node changed as result of this call?

Step 4:   What is the significance of the call to procedure ReverseNode in which parameter P is NIL?

Step 5:   Describe how the calls to procedure ReverseNode combine to reverse the list. Draw a diagram to illustrate your answer.

PART C

Passing a pointer variable using call-by-reference allows you to reconfigure the structure of lists in a straightforward manner. Consider the ListInsertLast procedure given below.

```
PROCEDURE ListInsertLast ( VAR L : List;
                               NewElement : ListElement );

{  Inserts NewElement at the end of list L.  }

    PROCEDURE InsertLastNode ( VAR P, CurrP : ListNodePtr;
                                   NewElement : ListElement     );
    BEGIN
    IF  P <> NIL
        THEN  InsertLastNode(P^.Next,CurrP,NewElement)
        ELSE  BEGIN
              New(P);
              P^.Element := NewElement;
              P^.Next    := NIL;
              CurrP      := P;
              END;
    END;

BEGIN
InsertLastNode(L.Head,L.Current,NewElement);
END;
```

 Step 1: Add the following statement to the test program in the file TEST8.PAS.

```
ListInsertLast(TestList,'!');
```

Step 2: Execute the ListInsertLast procedure using the following list.

```
TestList.Head  →  'A'  →  'B'  →  'C'  →  NIL
```

Step 3: What is the significance of the calls to procedure InsertLastNode in which P is *not* NIL?

Step 4:   Describe what each statement in procedure InsertLastNode does during the call in which parameter P is NIL. Draw a diagram to illustrate your answer.

Step 5:   What list does the ListInsertLast procedure produce when the call

    ListInsertLast(TestList,'!');

is made with the following empty list?

    TestList.Head → NIL

Describe how this result is accomplished. Draw a diagram to illustrate your answer.

PART D

You can use recursion with functions as well as with procedures. An example is the ListLength function given below.

```
FUNCTION ListLength ( L : List ) : INTEGER;

{  Returns the number of nodes in list L.  }

    FUNCTION SubListLength ( P : ListNodePtr ) : INTEGER;
    BEGIN
    IF P = NIL
       THEN SubListLength := 0
       ELSE SubListLength := SubListLength(P^.Next) + 1;
    END;

BEGIN
ListLength := SubListLength(L.Head);
END;
```

 Step 1:   Add the following statement to the test program in the file TEST8.PAS.

```
WRITELN('Length : ',ListLength(TestList));
```

Step 2:   Execute the ListLength function using the following list.

```
TestList.Head → 'A' → 'B' → 'C' → NIL
```

Step 3:   What is the significance of the call to function SubListLength in which parameter P is NIL?

Step 4: Describe how the calls to function SubListLength combine to return the length of the list. Draw a diagram to illustrate your answer.

Step 5: What value does the ListLength function return when called with the following empty list?

```
TestList.Head → NIL
```

Describe how this value is computed. Draw a diagram to illustrate your answer.

LABORATORY 8: In-lab Exercise 1

Date .... Section ....

Name ....

PART A

The following procedure from the file RECLIST.PAS performs some unspecified action.

```
PROCEDURE ListUnknown1 ( L : List );

{  Assumes that objects of type ListElement can be output  }
{  using a WRITE statement.                                 }

  PROCEDURE Unknown1Node ( P : ListNodePtr );
  BEGIN
  IF P <> NIL
     THEN BEGIN
          WRITE(P^.Element,' ');
          IF P^.Next <> NIL
             THEN BEGIN
                  Unknown1Node(P^.Next^.Next);
                  WRITE(P^.Next^.Element,' ');
                  END;
          END;
  END;

BEGIN
Unknown1Node(L.Head);
WRITELN;
END;
```

Step 1: Add the following statement to the test program in the file TEST8.PAS.

```
ListUnknown1(TestList);
```

Step 2: Execute the ListUnknown1 procedure using the following list.

```
TestList.Head → 'A' → 'B' → 'C' → 'D' → 'E' → NIL
```

Step 3:   What output is produced by this call to ListUnknown1?

Step 4:   Describe what each statement in procedure Unknown1Node does during the call in which parameter P points to the node containing 'A'.

Step 5:   Describe how the calls to procedure Unknown1Node combine to output the list. Draw a diagram to illustrate your answer.

PART B

The ListUnknown2 procedure in the file RECLIST.PAS performs yet another unspecified action.

```
PROCEDURE ListUnknown2 ( VAR L : List );

    PROCEDURE Unknown2Node ( VAR P : ListNodePtr );
    VAR Q : ListNodePtr;
    BEGIN
    IF P <> NIL
        THEN BEGIN
            Q := P;
            P := P^.Next;
            IF P <> NIL
                THEN Unknown2Node(P^.Next);
            DISPOSE(Q);
            END;
    END;

BEGIN
Unknown2Node(L.Head);
L.Current:=L.Head;
END;
```

Step 1: Add the following statement to the test program in the file TEST8.PAS.

```
ListUnknown2(TestList);
```

Step 2: Execute the ListUnknown2 procedure using the following list

```
TestList.Head → 'A' → 'B' → 'C' → 'D' → 'E' → NIL
```

Step 3: What list is produced by this call to ListUnknown2?

Step 4:   Describe what each statement in procedure Unknown2Node does during the call in which parameter P points to the node containing 'A'. In particular, what role does the fact that P is passed using call-by-reference play in this call?

Step 5:   Describe how the calls to procedure Unknown2Node combine to restructure the list. Draw a diagram to illustrate your answer.

LABORATORY 8: In-lab Exercise 2

Date .... Section ....

Name ....

Although recursion can be a powerful and intuitive means for expressing algorithms, there are times you may wish to replace recursion with iteration. This is most commonly done when analysis of a program's execution reveals that the overhead associated with a particular recursive routine is too costly, in terms of either time or memory usage.

PART A

Replacing recursion in a routine such as the ListLength function (Prelab Exercise, Part D) is fairly easy. Rather than using recursive calls to move through the list, you iterate through the list elements using a pointer (of type ListNodePtr). In the case of the ListLength function, you continue this iterative process until you reach the end of the list.

The ListReverse procedure (Prelab Exercise, Part B) presents a somewhat more challenging problem. The iterative form of this routine moves a set of pointers through the list in a coordinated manner. As these pointers move through the list, they reverse the links between pairs of nodes, thereby reversing the list itself.

Step 1:   Create a Pascal implementation of the ListReverse procedure that uses iteration, in conjunction with a small set of pointers, in place of recursion. Call this procedure ListIterReverse.

 Step 2:   Add your ListIterReverse procedure to the file RECLIST.PAS.

 Step 3:   Add the following statement to the test program in the file TEST8.PAS.

```
ListIterReverse(TestList);
```

Step 4:   Prepare a test plan for your ListIterReverse procedure that covers lists of different lengths, including lists containing a single element. A test plan form follows.

Step 5:   Execute your test plan. If you discover mistakes in your ListIterReverse procedure, correct them and execute your test plan again.

Test Plan for the ListIterReverse procedure			
Test case	*List*	*Expected result*	*Checked*

PART B

The ListWriteMirror procedure (Prelab Exercise, Part A) presents an even greater challenge. The iterative form of this routine incorporates a stack containing pointers to the nodes in the list. This stack is used in concert with an iterative process of the following form.

```
StackCreate(TempStack);

P := The head of the list.
WHILE P <> NIL DO                    {  Traverse from  }
    BEGIN                            {  first to last  }
    Push(TempStack,P);
    Process the list node pointed to by P (if necessary).
    P := P^.Next;
    END;

WHILE NOT StackEmpty(TempStack) DO   {  Traverse from  }
    BEGIN                            {  last to first  }
    Pop(TempStack,P);
    Process the list node pointed to by P.
    END;
```

Note that type StackElement is equivalent to type ListNodePtr, and that pointer P is of type ListNodePtr.

Step 1: Create a Pascal implementation of the ListWriteMirror procedure that uses iteration in conjunction with a stack, in place of recursion. Call the resulting procedure ListStkWriteMirror. Base your ListStkWriteMirror procedure on the following framework.

```
PROCEDURE ListStkWriteMirror ( L : List );

TYPE StackElement = ListNodePtr;
     {  Include the declarations in the file STACKxxx.DEC here.  }

VAR  TempStack : Stack;        {  Stack of list node pointers  }
     P          : ListNodePtr;  {  Pointer to list node          }

{  Include the routines in the file STACKxxx.PAS here.  }

BEGIN

{  Include the iterative process here.  }

END;
```

The files STACKxxx.DEC and STACKxxx.PAS used in this framework specify one of the stack implementations you created in Laboratory 4.

 Step 2:   Add your ListStkWriteMirror procedure to the file RECLIST.PAS.

 Step 3:   Add the following statement to the test program in the file TEST8.PAS.

```
ListStkWriteMirror(TestList);
```

Step 4:   Prepare a test plan for your ListStkWriteMirror procedure that covers lists of different lengths, including lists containing a single element.

Step 5:   Execute your test plan. If you discover mistakes in your ListStkWriteMirror procedure, correct them and execute your test plan again.

Test Plan for the ListStkWriteMirror procedure			
Test case	*List*	*Expected result*	*Checked*

LABORATORY 8: In-lab Exercise 3

Date .... Section ....

Name ....

You saw in the Prelab that recursion can support the insertion of list elements. You can also use recursion to express the restructuring required after the deletion of list elements.

PROCEDURE ListDeleteC (VAR L : List)

Requires:
List L has been created.

Results:
Removes all elements containing the character 'C' from L. The first element in the list (if any) becomes the current list element.

Step 1:   Create a Pascal implementation of this operation. Your implementation should be based on recursion, *not* iteration.

 Step 2:   Add your implementation of this operation to the file RECLIST.PAS.

 Step 3:   Add the following code to the test program in the file TEST8.PAS.

```
ListDeleteC(TestList);
```

Step 4:   Prepare a test plan for the ListDeleteC operation that includes lists containing the character 'C' at the beginning, middle, and end.

Step 5:   Execute your test plan. If you discover mistakes in your implementation of the ListDeleteC operation, correct them and execute your test plan again.

Test Plan for the ListDeleteC operation			
Test case	*List*	*Expected result*	*Checked*

LABORATORY 8: In-lab Exercise 4

Date .... Section ....

Name ....

You can use recursion to support the insertion of list elements in the middle of lists, as well as at the end of lists.

PROCEDURE ListABeforeB (VAR L : List)

Requires:
List L has been created.

Results:
Inserts an element containing the character 'A' immediately before each element in L containing the character 'B'. The current list element designation remains unchanged.

Step 1: Create a Pascal implementation of this operation. Your implementation should be based on recursion, *not* iteration.

Step 2: Add your implementation of this operation to the file RECLIST.PAS.

Step 3: Add the following code to the test program in the file TEST8.PAS.

```
ListABeforeB(TestList);
```

Step 4: Prepare a test plan for the ListABeforeB operation that includes lists containing the character 'B' at the beginning, middle, and end. A test plan form follows.

Step 5: Execute your test plan. If you discover mistakes in your implementation of the ListABeforeB operation, correct them and execute your test plan again.

Test Plan for the ListABeforeB operation			
Test case	List	Expected result	Checked

LABORATORY 8: Postlab Exercise 1

Date .... Section ....

Name ....

One mistake we sometimes make when we are first introduced to recursion is to use a WHILE-DO loop in place of an IF-THEN-ELSE selection structure. Suppose we replace the statement

```
IF P <> NIL
   THEN BEGIN
        WRITE(P^.Element);
        WriteMirrorNode(P^.Next);
        WRITE(P^.Element);
        END;
```

in the WriteMirrorNode procedure (Prelab Exercise, Part A) with the statement

```
WHILE P <> NIL DO
    BEGIN
    WRITE(P^.Element);
    WriteMirrorNode(P^.Next);
    WRITE(P^.Element);
    END;
```

What would be the consequence of this change?

LABORATORY 8: Postlab Exercise 2

Date .... Section ....

Name ....

It is often impossible to convert a recursive routine to iterative form without adding the use of a stack (see In-lab Exercise 2). Explain why a stack is needed by the iterative form of the ListWriteMirror procedure.

Expression Tree ADT

OVERVIEW

You customarily write arithmetic expressions in linear form. When you evaluate arithmetic expressions, however, you treat them as hierarchical entities. For example, when asked to evaluate the arithmetic expression

$$(1+3)*(6-4)$$

you begin by adding 1 to 3. Then you subtract 4 from 6. Finally, you multiply these intermediate results together to produce 8, the value of the expression.

In performing these calculations, you have implicitly formed a hierarchy in which the multiplication operator is built on a foundation consisting of the addition and subtraction operators. We can represent this hierarchy explicitly using the following binary tree. Trees such as this one are referred to as **expression trees**.

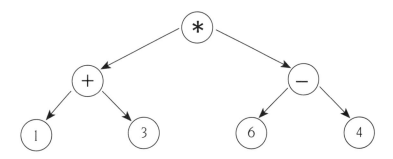

EXPRESSION TREE ADT

ELEMENTS
Each node in an expression tree contains either an arithmetic operator or a numeric value.

STRUCTURE
The nodes form a tree in which each node containing an arithmetic operator has a pair of children that correspond to that operator's operands. Each child is the root node of a subtree that represents the corresponding operand (or subexpression). Nodes containing numeric values have no children.

OPERATIONS

PROCEDURE ExprTreeBuild (VAR T : ExprTree)

Requires:
None.
Results:
Reads an arithmetic expression in prefix form from the keyboard and builds the corresponding expression tree T.

PROCEDURE ExprTreeExpression (T : ExprTree)

Requires:
Expression tree T has been built.
Results:
Outputs the arithmetic expression corresponding to T in fully parenthesized infix form.

FUNCTION ExprTreeEvaluate (T : ExprTree) : REAL

Requires:
Expression tree T is not empty.
Results:
Returns the value of the arithmetic expression corresponding to T.

PROCEDURE ExprTreeShowStructure (T : ExprTree)

Requires:
Expression tree T has been built.
Results:
Outputs T with its branches oriented from left (root) to right (leaves). That is, the tree is output rotated counterclockwise ninety degrees from its conventional orientation. If the tree is empty, outputs "Empty tree". This operation is intended for debugging purposes only. It assumes that arithmetic expressions contain only single-digit, nonnegative integers and the arithmetic operators for addition, substraction, multiplication, and division.

In Laboratory 4, In-lab Exercise 2, you examined the infix and postfix forms of arithmetic expressions. In the infix form of an arithmetic expression, each operator is placed between its operands; in the postfix form, each operator is placed immediately after its operands. In this laboratory, you focus on prefix form. Each operator in the prefix form of an arithmetic expression is placed immediately before its operands. For example, the arithmetic expression

$$(1+3)*(6-4)$$

is written in prefix form as

$$*+13-64$$

When processing the prefix form of an arithmetic expression from left to right, you will, by definition, encounter each operator followed by its operands. If you know in advance the number of operands that an operator has, you can use the following recursive process to construct the corresponding expression tree.

Read the next arithmetic operator or numeric value.
Create a node containing the operator or numeric value.
IF the node contains an operator
    THEN Recursively build the subtrees that correspond to the operator's operands.
    ELSE The node is a leaf node.

If you apply this process to the arithmetic expression

$$*+13-64$$

then construction of the corresponding expression tree proceeds as follows:

Read '*'

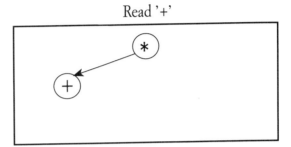

Read '+'

Read '1'

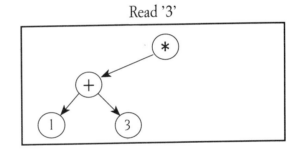

Read '3'

Read '–'

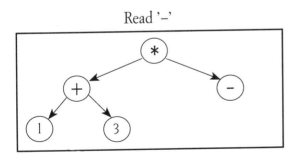

Read '6'

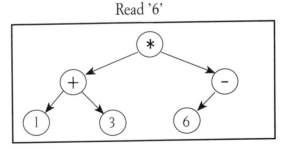

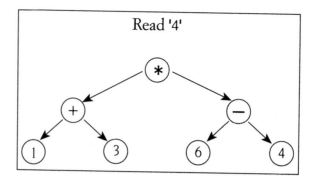

Note that in processing this arithmetic expression we have assumed that all numeric values are single-digit, nonnegative integers, and thus that all numeric values can be represented as single characters. If we were to generalize this process to include multidigit numbers, we would have to include delimiters in the expression to separate the digits in one number from the digits in the next.

LABORATORY 9: Cover Sheet

Date .... Section ....

Name ....

Place a check mark in the "Assigned" column next to the exercises your instructor has assigned to your class. Attach this cover sheet to the front of the packet of materials you submit following the laboratory.

	Assigned	*Completed*
Prelab Exercise	✓	
In-lab Exercise 1	✓	
In-lab Exercise 2		
In-lab Exercise 3		
In-lab Exercise 4		
Postlab Exercise 1		
Postlab Exercise 2		
		Total

LABORATORY 9: Prelab Exercise

Date .... Section ....

Name ....

As you saw in the Overview, the construction and evaluation of expression trees can easily be described using recursion. In this exercise, you explore the use of recursion in the implementation of these operations.

Step 1: Create a Pascal implementation of the Expression Tree ADT using a linked tree structure. Each node in the tree should contain a character (Element) and a pair of pointers to the node's children (Left and Right). Your implementation should maintain a pointer to the tree's root node (Root). Base your implementation on the following TYPE declarations.

```
ExprTreeNodePtr = ^ExprTreeNode;

ExprTreeNode    = RECORD
                     Element : CHAR;
                     Left,
                     Right   : ExprTreeNodePtr;
                  END;

ExprTree        = RECORD
                     Root : ExprTreeNodePtr;
                  END;
```

Assume that an arithmetic expression consists of

- single-digit, nonnegative integers ('0'..'9'), and

- the four basic arithmetic operators ('+', '−', '*' and '/').

Further assume that each arithmetic expression is input in prefix form from the keyboard with all characters on one line.

 An implementation of the ExprTreeShowStructure operation is given in the file SHOW9.PAS.

Step 2: Create a file called EXPRTREE.DEC that contains these TYPE declarations and a file called EXPRTREE.PAS that contains the routines in your implementation. Include comments that describe the linked representation of an expression tree and the operations in your implementation.

LABORATORY 9: In-lab Exercise 1

Date .... Section ....

Name ....

Test your implementation of the Expression Tree ADT using the test program in the file TEST9.PAS.

Step 1: Complete the following test plan by filling in the expected result for each arithmetic expression. You may wish to include additional arithmetic expressions in this test plan.

Step 2: Execute this test plan. If you discover mistakes in your implementation of the Expression Tree ADT, correct them and execute the test plan again.

Test Plan for the operations in the Expression Tree ADT			
Test case	*Arithmetic expression*	*Expected result*	*Checked*
One operator	+34		
Nested operators	*+34/52		
All operators at start	-/*9321		
Uneven nesting	*4+6-75		
Zero dividend	/02		
Single-digit number	7		

LABORATORY 9: In-lab Exercise 2

Date ....   Section ....

Name ....

Computers are composed of logic circuits that take a set of boolean input values and produce a boolean output. You can represent this mapping from inputs to output with a logic expression consisting of the boolean logic operators AND, OR, and NOT (defined below) and the boolean values True (T) and False (F).

A	(NOT) *-A*		*A*	*B*	(AND) *A∗B*	(OR) *A+B*
F	T		F	F	F	F
T	F		F	T	F	T
			T	F	F	T
			T	T	T	T

Just as you can construct an arithmetic expression tree from an arithmetic expression, you can construct a logic expression tree from a logic expression. For example, the following logic expression

$$(T∗F)+(T∗–F)$$

can be expressed in prefix form as

$$+∗TF∗T–F$$

Applying the expression tree construction process described in the Prelab to this expression produces the following logic expression tree.

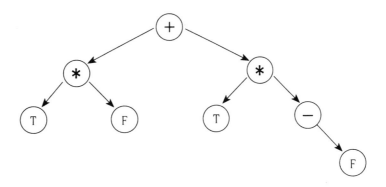

Evaluating this tree yields the boolean value True (T).

Note that constructing this tree requires processing a unary operator, the boolean operator NOT. When building a logic expression tree, the right child of any node containing the NOT operator should be set to point to the operand, and the left child should be set to NIL. Be careful when performing the remaining operations so you avoid traversing these NIL left children.

Step 1: Create an implementation of the Expression Tree ADT that supports logic expressions consisting of the boolean values True and False ('T' and 'F') and the boolean operators AND, OR, and NOT ('*', '+', and '−'). Change the definition of the ExprTreeEvaluate operation so it yields a BOOLEAN value rather than a REAL value.

Step 2: Create a file called LOGITREE.DEC that contains the TYPE declarations in the file EXPRTREE.DEC, and a file called LOGITREE.PAS that contains the routines in your implementation of the Logic Expression Tree ADT.

Step 3: Modify the test program in the file TEST9.PAS so it includes the declarations and routines for your implementation of the Logic Expression Tree ADT (LOGITREE.DEC and LOGITREE.PAS) in place of those for the Arithmetic Expression Tree ADT.

Step 4: Complete the following test plan by filling in the expected result for each logic expression. You may wish to include additional logic expressions in this test plan.

Step 5: Execute this test plan. If you discover mistakes in your implementation of the Logic Expression Tree ADT, correct them and execute the test plan again.

Test Plan for the Logic Expression Tree ADT			
Test case	*Logic expression*	*Expected result*	*Checked*
One operator	+TF		
Nested operators	*+TF+FT		
NOT (logic value)	+*TF*T−F		
NOT (subexpression)	+−T−*TT		
NOT (nested expression)	−*+TTF		
Double negation	−−T		
Logic value	T		

Having produced a tool that constructs and evaluates logic expression trees, you can use this tool to investigate the use of logic circuits to perform binary arithmetic. Suppose you have two one-bit binary numbers (X and Y). You can add these numbers together to produce a one-bit sum (S) and a one-bit carry (C). The results of one-bit binary addition for all combinations of X and Y are tabulated below.

		X	*Y*	*C*	*S*
	X	0	0	0	0
+	Y	0	1	0	1
	C S	1	0	0	1
		1	1	1	0

If you interpret 1 as True and 0 as False, then you can use the following logic expressions to compute the values of S and C from the input values of X and Y.

$$C = *XY \qquad S = +*X{-}Y*{-}XY$$

Step 6:   Using your implementation of the Logic Expression Tree ADT and the (modified) test program, confirm that these logic expressions are correct by completing the following table.

X	*Y*	*C* = *XY	*S* = +*X–Y*–XY
F	F	*FF =	+*F–F*–FF =
F	T	*FT =	+*F–T*–FT =
T	F	*TF =	+*T–F*–TF =
T	T	*TT =	+*T–T*–TT =

LABORATORY 9: In-lab Exercise 3

Date .... Section ....

Name ....

An algebraic formula is an arithmetic expression that contains variables as well as arithmetic operators and numeric values. Given the following algebraic formula in infix form (where B and H denote variables)

$$(1/2)*(B*H)$$

the corresponding expression tree is

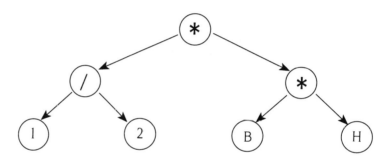

In order to evaluate an algebraic formula, the variables in the formula must be assigned numeric values. You can use an array of type VarList to pair single-character variable names with real number values.

```
TYPE VarList = ARRAY ['A'..'Z'] OF REAL;
```

The contents of an array FormulaVars of type VarList are interpreted as follows:

```
FormulaVars['A']  contains the value of variable A
FormulaVars['B']  contains the value of variable B
                  • • •
FormulaVars['Z']  contains the value of variable Z
```

The contents of this array are needed in order to evaluate an algebraic formula. Thus, this array must be passed to the ExprTreeEvaluate operation along with the formula's expression tree. A specification of the ExprTreeEvaluate operation that incorporates this change is given below.

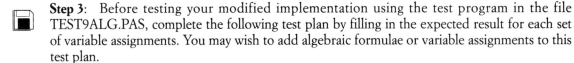

```
FUNCTION ExprTreeEvaluate ( T : ExprTree;
                            FormulaVars : VarList ) : REAL
```

Requires:
Expression tree T is not empty, and FormulaVars pairs each variable in T with a numeric value.
Results:
Returns the value of the algebraic formula corresponding to T.

Step 1: Modify your implementation of the Expression Tree ADT so that you can use it to manipulate algebraic formulae. Your modified implementation should support single-character variable names in addition to arithmetic operators and single-digit, nonnegative integers.

Step 2: Create a file called ALGTREE.DEC that includes the TYPE declaration for VarList along with the TYPE declarations in the file EXPRTREE.DEC. Create a file called ALGTREE.PAS that contains the routines in your modified implementation of the Expression Tree ADT.

Step 3: Before testing your modified implementation using the test program in the file TEST9ALG.PAS, complete the following test plan by filling in the expected result for each set of variable assignments. You may wish to add algebraic formulae or variable assignments to this test plan.

Step 4: Execute this test plan. If you discover mistakes in your modified implementation of the Expression Tree ADT, correct them and execute the test plan again.

Test Plan for the Expression Tree ADT (with algebraic formulae)			
Algebraic formula	*Variable assignments*	*Expected result*	*Checked*
*/12*BH	B=3 H=4		
*A+/BCD	A=3 B=11 C=2 D=4		
*A+/BCD	A=0.5 B=18 C=3 D=2		
X	X=0.25		

LABORATORY 9: In-lab Exercise 4

Date .... Section ....

Name ....

Commuting the operators in an expression requires restructuring the corresponding expression tree. For example, commuting *every* operator in the expression tree

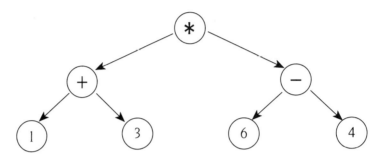

yields the expression tree

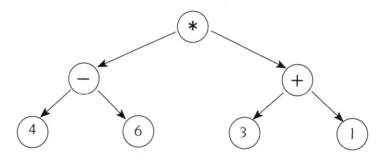

An operation for commuting expression trees is described below.

PROCEDURE ExprTreeCommute (VAR T : ExprTree)

Requires:
Expression tree T has been built.
Results:
Commutes the operands of every arithmetic operator in the expression tree.

Step 1: Create a Pascal implementation of this operation.

Step 2: Add your implementation of this operation to the file EXPRTREE.PAS.

 Step 3: Add the following code to the test program in the file TEST9.PAS.

```
ExprTreeCommute(Expression);
ExprTreeShowStructure(Expression);
ExprTreeExpression(Expression);
WRITELN(' = ',ExprTreeEvaluate(Expression));
```

Step 4: Prepare a test plan for the ExprTreeCommute operation that includes a variety of arithmetic expressions.

Step 5: Execute your test plan. If you discover mistakes in your implementation of the ExprTreeCommute operation, correct them and execute your test plan again.

Test Plan for the ExprTreeCommute operation			
Test case	*Arithmetic expression*	*Expected result*	*Checked*

Date .... Section ....

Name ....

What type of traversal (inorder, preorder, or postorder) serves as the basis of your implementation of each of the following Expression Tree ADT operations? Briefly explain why you used a given traversal to implement a particular operation.

ExprTreeBuild   Traversal:

Explanation:

ExprTreeExpression   Traversal:

Explanation:

ExprTreeEvaluate   Traversal:

Explanation:

LABORATORY 9: Postlab Exercise 2

Date .... Section ....

Name ....

Consider the procedures ExprTreeWrite1 and ExprTreeWrite2 given below.

```
PROCEDURE ExprTreeWrite1 ( T : ExprTree );
    PROCEDURE WriteNode1 ( P : ExprTreeNodePtr );
    BEGIN
    IF P <> NIL
       THEN BEGIN
            WriteNode1(P^.Left);
            WRITE(P^.Element);
            WriteNode1(P^.Right);
            END;
    END;
BEGIN
IF T.Root <> NIL THEN WriteNode1(T.Root);
END;
PROCEDURE ExprTreeWrite2 ( T : ExprTree );
    PROCEDURE WriteNode2 ( P : ExprTreeNodePtr );
    BEGIN
    IF P^.Left <> NIL THEN WriteNode2(P^.Left);
    WRITE(P^.Element);
    IF P^.Right <> NIL THEN WriteNode2(P^.Right);
    END;
BEGIN
IF T.Root <> NIL THEN WriteNode2(T.Root);
END;
```

When called using the same expression tree, will these procedures produce the same output? If not, why not? If so, how do the procedures differ and why might this difference be important?

Binary Search Tree ADT

OVERVIEW

In Laboratory 9, you saw how the evaluation of an arithmetic expression could be represented using a hierarchical data structure, the expression tree. In this laboratory, you examine how a binary tree can be used to represent the hierarchical search process embodied in the binary search algorithm.

You can use the binary search algorithm to efficiently locate an element in an array, provided that each element in the array has a unique key (identifier) and that the array elements are stored in order based on their keys. Given the following array of keys,

	1	2	3	4	5	6	7
Key	16	20	31	43	65	72	86

a binary search for the element with key 31 begins by comparing 31 with the key in the middle of the array, 43. Because 31 is less than 43, the element with key 31 must lie in the lower half of the array (entries 1–3). The key in the middle of this subarray is 20. Because 31 is greater than 20, the element with key 31 must lie in the upper half of this subarray (entry 3). This array entry contains the key 31. Thus, the search terminates with success.

Although the comparisons made during a search for a given key depend on the key, the order in which comparisons are made is invariant for a given array of elements. For instance, when searching through the preceeding array, you always compare the key you are searching for with 43 before you compare it with either 20 or 72. Similarly, you always compare the key you are searching for with 72 before you compare it with either 65 or 86. The order of comparisons associated with this array is shown in the following table.

	1	2	3	4	5	6	7
Key	16	20	31	43	65	72	86
Order compared	3	2	3	1	3	2	3

The hierarchical nature of the comparisons that are performed during the binary search process is reflected in the following tree.

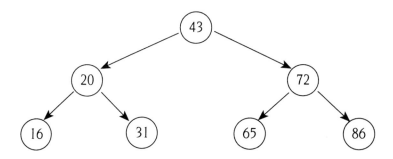

Note that for each key K in this tree, all of the keys in K's left subtree are less than K and all of the keys in K's right subtree are greater than K. Trees with this property are called **binary search trees**.

BINARY SEARCH TREE ADT

ELEMENTS
Each element in a binary search tree has a key that uniquely identifies it. Elements usually include additional data.

STRUCTURE
The elements form a binary tree. For each element E in the tree, all elements in E's left subtree have keys that are less than E's key, and all elements in E's right subtree have keys that are greater than E's key.

OPERATIONS

PROCEDURE BSTreeCreate (VAR T : BSTree)

Requires:
None.
Results:
Creates an empty binary search tree T.

PROCEDURE BSTreeInsert (VAR T : BSTree;
                          NewElement : BSTreeElement)

Requires:
Binary search tree T is not full.
Results:
Inserts element NewElement into T. If an element with the same key as NewElement already exists in T, then updates that element's nonkey fields with NewElement's nonkey fields.

```
FUNCTION BSTreeRetrieve ( T : BSTree;
                          SrchKey : BSTreeKey;
                          VAR SrchElement : BSTreeElement )
                                                   : BOOLEAN
```

Requires:
Binary search tree T has been created.
Results:
Searches T for the element with key SrchKey. If this element is found, then returns true with SrchElement returning the element. Otherwise, returns false with SrchElement undefined.

```
FUNCTION BSTreeDelete ( VAR T : BSTree;
                        DelKey : BSTreeKey ) : BOOLEAN
```

Requires:
Binary search tree T has been created.
Results:
Deletes the element with key DelKey from T. Returns true if this element exists (and is deleted). Otherwise, returns false.

```
PROCEDURE BSTreeWriteAscending ( T : BSTree )
```

Requires:
Binary search tree T has been created.
Results:
Outputs the elements in T in ascending order based on their keys. Uses a call to procedure WriteBSTreeElement to output each element. Procedure WriteBSTreeElement must be part of any program that uses the Binary Search Tree ADT.

```
FUNCTION BSTreeEmpty ( T : BSTree ) : BOOLEAN
```

Requires:
Binary search tree T has been created.
Results:
If T is empty, then returns true. Otherwise, returns false.

```
FUNCTION BSTreeFull ( T : BSTree ) : BOOLEAN
```

Requires:
Binary search tree T has been created.
Results:
If T is full, then returns true. Otherwise, returns false.

```
PROCEDURE BSTreeClear ( VAR T : BSTree )
```

Requires:
Binary search tree T has been created.
Results:
Deletes all elements in T.

PROCEDURE BSTreeShowStructure (T : BSTree)

Requires:
Binary search tree T has been created.

Results:
Outputs T with its branches oriented from left (root) to right (leaves). If the tree is empty, outputs "Empty tree". This operation is intended for debugging purposes only. It assumes that keys will produce no more than three characters when output.

LABORATORY 10: Cover Sheet

Date .... Section ....

Name ....

Place a check mark in the "Assigned" column next to the exercises your instructor has assigned to your class. Attach this cover sheet to the front of the packet of materials you submit following the laboratory.

	Assigned	*Completed*
Prelab Exercise	✓	
In-lab Exercise 1	✓	
In-lab Exercise 2		
In-lab Exercise 3		
In-lab Exercise 4		
Postlab Exercise 1		
Postlab Exercise 2		
		Total

LABORATORY 10: Prelab Exercise

Date .... Section ....

Name ....

When you search for a key in a binary search tree, you begin at the root node and progress downward along a branch until you either find the key or you reach a leaf node without finding the key. As you encounter nodes, you move down to the left if the key you are searching for is less than the key stored in a node; you move down to the right if the key you are searching for is greater than the key stored in a node. Each step downward along a branch corresponds to an array subdivision in the binary search algorithm.

Step 1:   Create a Pascal implementation of the Binary Search Tree ADT using a linked tree structure. Each node in the tree should contain an element (Element) with a unique key (Element.Key) and a pair of pointers to the node's children (Left and Right). Your implementation should maintain a pointer to the tree's root node (Root). Base your implementation on the following TYPE declarations.

```
BSTreeNodePtr = ^BSTreeNode;

BSTreeNode    = RECORD
                   Element : BSTreeElement;
                   Left,
                   Right   : BSTreeNodePtr;
                END;

BSTree        = RECORD
                   Root : BSTreeNodePtr;
                END;
```

Note that TYPE declarations of the following form must appear in any program that uses the Binary Search Tree ADT.

```
BSTreeKey     = ...
BSTreeElement = RECORD
                   Key : BSTreeKey;
                   ...
                END;
```

Assume that BSTreeKey is a type that can be compared using the standard comparison operators ('<', '=', etc.).

An implementation of the BSTreeShowStructure operation is given in the file SHOW10.PAS.

Step 2:   Create a file called BSTREE.DEC that contains the BSTreeNodePtr, BSTreeNode, and BSTree TYPE declarations and a file called BSTREE.PAS that contains the routines in your implementation. Include comments that describe the linked tree representation of a binary search tree and the operations in your implementation.

LABORATORY 10: In-lab Exercise 1

Date .... Section ....

Name ....

 The test program in the file TEST10.PAS allows you to interactively test your implementation of the Binary Search Tree ADT using the following commands.

Command	Action
+key	Insert (or update) the element with the specified key.
?key	Retrieve the element with the specified key and output it.
–key	Delete the element with the specified key.
A	Output all elements in ascending key order.
E	Report whether the tree is empty.
F	Report whether the tree is full.
C	Clear the tree.
Q	Quit the test program.

Step 1:   Prepare a test plan for your implementation of the Binary Search Tree ADT. Your test plan should cover trees of various shapes and sizes, including empty, single-branch, and single-element trees. A test plan form follows.

Step 2:   Execute your test plan. If you discover mistakes in your implementation, correct them and execute your test plan again.

Test Plan for the operations in the Binary Search Tree ADT			
Test case	*Commands*	*Expected result*	*Checked*

LABORATORY 10: In-lab Exercise 2

A database that contains a set of account records of the following form

```
AcctID     = INTEGER;
AcctRecord = RECORD
               ID        : AcctID;
               FirstName : ARRAY [1..10] OF CHAR;
               LastName  : ARRAY [1..15] OF CHAR;
               Balance   : REAL;
            END;
```

typically is stored in a direct-access file. Each record in a direct-access file is assigned a record number based on that record's position within the file.

Record number	Contents
1	1st account record
2	2nd account record
...	...
N	Nth account record

You can use a record number to retrieve an account record directly (that is, without going through the entire file from the beginning) much as you can use an array index to reference an array element directly.

Unfortunately, record numbers are assigned by the file mechanism and are not part of the account information. As a result, they are not meaningful to users of the accounts database. Instead of retrieving account records using record numbers, database users prefer to retrieve account records using the database key, the account ID field. To support this type of retrieval you need to construct an index that relates account IDs and record numbers. You can implement this index using a binary search tree in which each element contains two fields: an account ID and a record number. The following TYPE declarations define this index tree.

```
BSTreeKey     = AcctID;
BSTreeElement = RECORD
                  Key    : BSTreeKey;
                  RecNum : INTEGER;
                END;
```

You construct an index tree by inserting an element into the tree for each account record in the database. For example, inserting the following account records

Record #	Account ID	First name	Last name	Balance
1	6274	James	Johnson	415.56
2	2843	Marcus	Wilson	9217.23
3	4892	Maureen	Albright	1462.56
4	8337	Debra	Douglas	27.26
5	1892	Bruce	Gold	719.32
6	9523	John	Carlson	1496.24

into an empty index tree yields the index tree shown below.

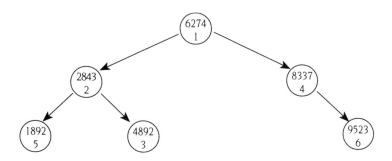

Given an account ID, retrieval of the corresponding account record is a two-step process:

- First, you retrieve the element in the index tree that has the specified account ID.

- Then, using the record number stored in this index element, you retrieve the corresponding account record from the database file.

The result is an efficient retrieval process that is based on an account's ID rather than its record number.

 Step 1: Using the program shell given in the file DBSHELL.PAS as a basis, create a Pascal program that builds an index tree for an accounts database, and uses this index tree to perform the following functions.

- Output the account records in the database in ascending order based on their account IDs.

- Read an account ID from the keyboard and output the corresponding account record.

Standard Pascal does not support direct-access files. Thus, you need to use another direct-access structure, an array, to simulate a direct-access file.

```
AcctDB : ARRAY [ 1..100 ] OF AcctRecord;
```

 Begin by reading the accounts database in the text file ACCTFILE.DAT into the AcctDB array using the following code fragment.

```
RecNum := 0;
WHILE NOT EOF(AcctFile) DO
    BEGIN
    RecNum := RecNum + 1;
    READ(AcctFile,AcctDB[RecNum].ID);
    FOR J := 1 TO 10 DO
        READ(AcctFile,AcctDB[RecNum].FirstName[J]);
    FOR J := 1 TO 15 DO
        READ(AcctFile,AcctDB[RecNum].LastName[J]);
    READLN(AcctFile,AcctDB[RecNum].Balance);
    {  Insert the ( Account ID, RecNum ) pair into the  }
    {  index tree.                                      }
    END;
```

As each account record is added to the array, insert the corresponding index element into the index tree. Once the index tree has been constructed, use it to output the account records and to retrieve (and output) the user-specified account record.

Note that performing these output operations requires a WriteBSTreeElement procedure that takes an index element and outputs the corresponding account record (array entry). This routine will need to refer to the AcctDB array as a global variable.

 Step 2: Test your program using the accounts database in the text file ACCTFILE.DAT. Try to retrieve several account IDs, including account IDs that do *not* occur in the database.

LABORATORY 10: In-lab Exercise 3

Date .... Section ....

Name ....

You have created operations that allow you to retrieve a single element from a binary search tree and output all elements in a tree. The following operation allows you to output those elements whose keys lie within a specified range.

```
PROCEDURE BSTreeWriteLessThan ( T : BSTree;
                                SrchKey : BSTreeKey )
```

Requires:
Binary search tree T has been created.
Results:
Outputs the elements in T that have keys that are less than SrchKey. Note that SrchKey need not be a key in T. These elements are output in ascending order based on their keys. Uses a call to procedure WriteBSTreeElement to output each element.

You could implement this operation using an inorder traversal in which you search through the entire tree, comparing keys with SrchKey and outputting those elements whose keys are less than SrchKey. Although successful, this approach is inefficient. It searches subtrees you know cannot possibly contain keys that are less than SrchKey.

Suppose that you are given a SrchKey value of 37 and the following binary search tree.

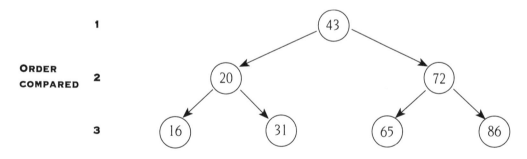

Since the root node has the key 43, you can immediately determine that you do not need to search (traverse) the root node's right subtree looking for keys that are less than 37. Similarly, if the value of SrchKey were 67, you would need to search the root node's right subtree, but would not need to search the right subtree of the node with key 72. Your implementation of the BSTreeWriteLessThan operation should use this idea to limit the portion of the tree that must be searched.

Step 1:   Create a Pascal implementation of the BSTreeWriteLessThan operation.

Step 2:   Add your implementation of this operation to the file BSTREE.PAS.

 Step 3:   Add the following code to the test program in the file TEST10.PAS.

```
ELSE IF Cmd = '<'
   THEN BEGIN
        WRITELN;
        WRITELN('Elements w/ key < ',InputKey,' :');
        BSTreeWriteLessThan(TestTree,InputKey);
        WRITELN('End of element list');
        END
```

You also must change the statement

```
IF ( Cmd = '+' ) OR ( Cmd = '?' ) OR ( Cmd = '-' )
   THEN READLN(InputKey)
   ELSE READLN;
```

to the statement

```
IF ( Cmd = '+' ) OR ( Cmd = '?' ) OR
   ( Cmd = '-' ) OR ( Cmd = '<' )
   THEN READLN(InputKey)
   ELSE READLN;
```

so you can specify the key to be used with the BSTreeWriteLessThan operation.

Step 4:   Prepare a test plan for this operation that covers a variety of trees and a variety of values for SrchKey, including values for SrchKey that do *not* occur in a particular tree. Be sure to include test cases that limit searches to the left subtree of the root node, the left subtree and part of the right subtree of the root node, the leftmost branch in the tree, and the entire tree. A test plan form follows.

Step 5:   Execute your test plan. If you discover mistakes in your implementation of the BSTreeWriteLessThan operation, correct them and execute your test plan again.

Test Plan for the BSTreeWriteLessThan operation			
Test case	*Commands*	*Expected result*	*Checked*

LABORATORY 10: In-lab Exercise 4

Date .... Section ....

Name ....

Binary search trees containing the same elements can vary widely in shape depending on the order in which the elements were inserted into each tree. One measurement of a tree's shape, its height, is of particular importance. The **height** of a binary search tree is the number of nodes on the longest path from the root node to any leaf node. This statistic is important because the amount of time that it can take to search for an element in a tree is a function of the height of the tree.

FUNCTION BSTreeHeight (T : BSTree) : INTEGER

Requires:
Binary search tree T has been created.
Results:
Returns the height of T.

You can compute the height of a tree T using a postorder traversal of the tree. For each node N in the tree, compute MaxLen(N), the length of the longest path from node N to any leaf node. MaxLen(N) can be computed as follows:

- If N is a leaf node, then MaxLen(N) = 1.

- Otherwise, MaxLen(N) = 1 + the greater of MaxLen(N^.Left) and MaxLen(N^.Right).

MaxLen(T.Root) is the height of tree T. It may be helpful if you return a value of 0 for MaxLen(NIL).

Step 1: Create a Pascal implementation of this operation.

Step 2: Add your implementation of this operation to the file BSTREE.PAS.

 Step 3: Add the following code to the test program in the file TEST10.PAS.

```
ELSE IF ( Cmd = 'H' ) OR ( Cmd = 'h' )
   THEN WRITELN('Tree height = ',BSTreeHeight(TestTree))
```

Step 4: Prepare a test plan for this operation that covers trees of various shapes and sizes, including empty and single-branch trees.

Step 5: Execute your test plan. If you discover mistakes in your implementation of the BSTreeHeight operation, correct them and execute your test plan again.

Test Plan for the BSTreeHeight operation			
Test case	*Commands*	*Expected result*	*Checked*

LABORATORY 10: Postlab Exercise 1

Date .... Section ....

Name ....

Given a set of N distinct keys, what are the heights of the shortest and tallest binary search trees that can be constructed from these keys? Give examples that illustrate your answer.

LABORATORY 10: Postlab Exercise 2

Date .... Section ....

Name ....

Given the shortest possible binary search tree containing N distinct keys, develop worst-case, order-of-magnitude estimates of the execution time of the following Binary Search Tree ADT operations. Briefly explain your reasoning behind each estimate.

BSTreeRetrieve   O(   )

Explanation:

BSTreeInsert   O(   )

Explanation:

BSTreeDelete   O(   )

Explanation:

BSTreeWriteAscending   O(   )

Explanation:

B-tree ADT

OVERVIEW

You can construct many different binary search trees from a given set of N elements. Depending on the order in which the elements are inserted, the height of the resulting tree can vary from $\log_2(N)$ to N. This wide variation in height is significant because, as you saw in Laboratory 10, the performance of many operations in the Binary Search Tree ADT is directly related to the height of the tree to which they are applied.

In this laboratory, you examine the **B-tree,** a search tree in which each node contains multiple elements and growth takes place from the leaves upward toward the root, rather than downward away from the root. These combined properties produce a search tree of height O(logN), irrespective of the order in which elements are inserted into the tree.

The relationship between the elements in a B-tree is a generalization of the relationship that exists in binary search trees.

- Let $E_1, E_2, \ldots, E_j$ denote the set of elements in a given B-tree node. For each element E_i in the node, E_i's key is greater than element E_{i-1}'s key and less than element E_{i+1}'s key. That is, the elements in a B-tree node are stored in ascending order according to their keys.

- Let $S_0, S_1, \ldots, S_j$ denote the set of subtrees for this node. For each element E_i in the node, all keys in subtree S_{i-1} are less than E_i's key, and all keys in subtree S_i are greater than E_i's key.

The search process used with B-trees is similar to the search process you used with binary search trees. Once again, each search begins with the root node and progresses downward along a branch. At each node along the branch, you perform the following steps.

- Check whether the key you are searching for matches the key of one of the elements stored in the node. If it does, then terminate the search with success.

- If the key is not in the node and the node is not a leaf node, then move down one level in the tree to the root node of the subtree that might contain the key. If the node is a leaf node, then terminate the search with failure.

Suppose you wish to search the B-tree shown below for the element with key 48. You begin by looking in the root node. This key is not stored in the root node, so you move down one level to the root node of the subtree containing keys between 27 and 52. This key is not stored in this node either, so you continue downward once again to the root node of the subtree containing keys greater than 41. The element with key 48 is stored in this node, and the search terminates with success. The resulting search path is highlighted by the dashed line in the following figure.

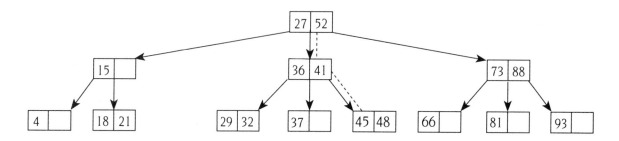

Because the branches in a B-tree are short, B-trees are particularly well-suited to an environment in which the tree is stored on disk rather than in memory. Short branches imply that fewer disk accesses will be needed to complete a search. Because disk accesses are slow (relative to the speed of a computer's processor and memory), fewer disk accesses produce a faster search.

B-TREE ADT

ELEMENTS
Each element in a B-tree has a key that uniquely identifies that element. Elements usually include additional data.

STRUCTURE
Each node in a B-tree contains up to M elements, $E_1, E_2, \ldots, E_M$, stored in ascending order according to their keys. The nodes form a tree in which each node has up to M+1 subtrees, $S_0, S_1, \ldots, S_M$. For each element E_i in a given node, all keys in subtree S_{i-1} are less than E_i's key, and all keys in subtree S_i are greater than E_i's key.

OPERATIONS

PROCEDURE BTreeCreate (VAR T : BTree)

Requires:
None.
Results:
Creates an empty B-tree T.

PROCEDURE BTreeInsert (VAR T : BTree;
                         NewElement : BTreeElement)

Requires:
B-tree T is not full.
Results:
Inserts element NewElement into T. If an element with the same key as NewElement already exists in T, then updates that element's nonkey fields with NewElement's nonkey fields.

```
FUNCTION BTreeRetrieve ( T : BTree;
                         SrchKey : BTreeKey;
                         VAR SrchElement : BTreeElement ) : BOOLEAN
```

Requires:
B-tree T has been created.

Results:
Searches T for the element with key SrchKey. If this element is found, then returns true with SrchElement returning the element. Otherwise, returns false with SrchElement undefined.

```
PROCEDURE BTreeWriteAscending ( T : BTree )
```

Requires:
B-tree T has been created.

Results:
Outputs the elements in T in ascending order according to their keys. Uses a call to procedure WriteBTreeElement to output each element. Procedure WriteBTreeElement must be part of any program that uses the B-tree ADT.

```
FUNCTION BTreeEmpty ( T : BTree ) : BOOLEAN
```

Requires:
B-tree T has been created.

Results:
If T is empty, then returns true. Otherwise, returns false.

```
FUNCTION BTreeFull ( T : BTree ) : BOOLEAN
```

Requires:
B-tree T has been created.

Results:
If T is full, then returns true. Otherwise, returns false.

```
PROCEDURE BTreeClear ( VAR T : BTree )
```

Requires:
B-tree T has been created.

Results:
Deletes all elements in T.

```
PROCEDURE BTreeShowStructure ( T : BTree )
```

Requires:
B-tree T has been created.

Results:
Outputs T with its branches oriented from left (root) to right (leaves). If the tree is empty, outputs "Empty tree". This operation is intended for debugging purposes only. It assumes that keys will produce no more than three characters when output.

LABORATORY 11: Cover Sheet

Date .... Section ....

Name ....

Place a check mark in the "Assigned" column next to the exercises your instructor has assigned to your class. Attach this cover sheet to the front of the packet of materials you submit following the laboratory.

	Assigned	*Completed*
Prelab Exercise	✓	
In-lab Exercise 1	✓	
In-lab Exercise 2		
In-lab Exercise 3		
In-lab Exercise 4		
Postlab Exercise 1		
Postlab Exercise 2		
		Total

LABORATORY 11: Prelab Exercise

Date .... Section ....

Name ....

This exercise focuses on the creation of an implementation of the B-tree ADT in which the B-tree nodes are stored in memory.

Step 1:   Create a Pascal implementation of the B-tree ADT using a linked tree structure. Each node in the tree should contain an array of elements (Element) and an array of pointers to the node's children (Child). Your implementation should maintain a pointer to the tree's root node (Root). Base your implementation on the following TYPE declarations.

```
BTreeNodePtr = ^BTreeNode;

BTreeNode    = RECORD
                  Size    : 0..MaxBTreeNodeSize;
                  Element : ARRAY [1..MaxBTreeNodeSize]
                                         OF BTreeElement;
                  Child   : ARRAY [0..MaxBTreeNodeSize]
                                         OF BTreeNodePtr;
               END;


BTree        = RECORD
                  Root : BTreeNodePtr;
               END;
```

A CONST declaration defining MaxBTreeNodeSize and TYPE declarations of the following form must appear in any program that uses the B-tree ADT.

```
BTreeKey     = ...
BTreeElement = RECORD
                  Key : BTreeKey;
                  ...
               END;
```

Assume that BTreeKey is a type that can be compared using the standard comparison operators ('<', '=', etc.).

An implementation of the BTreeCreate and BTreeInsert operations is given in the file BTREEINS.PAS. An implementation of the BTreeShowStructure operation is given in the file SHOW11.PAS.

Step 2:   Create a file called BTREE.DEC that contains the BTreeNodePtr, BTreeNode, and BTree TYPE declarations, and a file called BTREE.PAS that contains the routines in your implementation. Include comments that describe the linked tree representation of a B-tree and the operations in your implementation.

LABORATORY 11: In-lab Exercise 1

Date .... Section ....

Name ....

 The test program in the file TEST11.PAS allows you to interactively test your implementation of the B-tree ADT using the following commands.

Command	Action
+key	Insert (or update) the element with the specified key.
?key	Retrieve the element with the specified key and output it.
A	Output all elements in ascending key order.
E	Report whether the tree is empty.
F	Report whether the tree is full.
C	Clear the tree.
Q	Quit the test program.

Step 1: Prepare a test plan for your implementation of the B-tree ADT. Your test plan should cover trees of various shapes and sizes, including empty, single-branch, and single-element trees. A test plan form follows.

Step 2: Execute your test plan. If you discover mistakes in your implementation, correct them and execute your test plan again.

Step 3: Change the value of the constant MaxBTreeNodeSize to 2 (in the test program).

Step 4: Execute your test plan. If you discover mistakes in your implementation, correct them and execute your test plan again.

Test Plan for the operations in the B-tree ADT			
Test case	*Commands*	*Expected result*	*Checked*

Date .... Section ....

Name ....

Account activity pairs such as those shown below arise in a variety of settings. In a bank, they might represent customer account numbers and transaction amounts. In a real estate office, they might represent property account numbers and the dollar amounts bid on those properties (in thousands of dollars and without a negative value, of course).

Account ID	Amount
1548	840.29
5403	63.90
1548	1421.76
4892	−100.00
7145	270.00
1548	917.36
5403	81.50

In any case, if this information is to prove useful, you need to represent it in a form that more clearly relates each account with its associated amounts. One such form is an **account activity report** such as the one shown below.

Account ID	Activity		
1548	840.29	1421.76	917.36
4892	−100.00		
5403	63.90	81.50	
7145	270.00		

The accounts in this activity report are listed in ascending order based on their account IDs. The amounts associated with a given account are listed beside that account's ID number in the same order in which they appear in the set of account activity pairs.

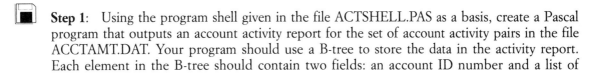

Step 1:   Using the program shell given in the file ACTSHELL.PAS as a basis, create a Pascal program that outputs an account activity report for the set of account activity pairs in the file ACCTAMT.DAT. Your program should use a B-tree to store the data in the activity report. Each element in the B-tree should contain two fields: an account ID number and a list of amounts.

Begin by creating an empty B-tree. Then, for each account activity pair in the file ACCTAMT.DAT, check whether the account is stored in the tree. If it is, add the amount value in the activity pair to the list of amounts associated with the account. If it is not, insert a new B-tree element for the account into the tree. The list of amounts in this newly inserted element should contain only the amount value in the activity pair.

Once you have constructed the B-tree, you can output the account activity report by invoking the BTreeWriteAscending operation. Note that outputting a line in the report requires a WriteBTreeElement procedure that takes a B-tree element and outputs both the account ID and the associated list of amounts. This list should be traversed using the operations in the List ADT. Include *one* of your implementations of the List ADT from Laboratories 2, 3, or 5. Base your program on the following TYPE declarations.

```
AcctID       = INTEGER;

ListElement  = REAL;
{  Include the TYPE declarations in the file LISTxxx.DEC here.  }

BTreeKey     = AcctID;
BTreeElement = RECORD
                  Key     : BTreeKey;
                  AmtList : List;
               END;
{  Include the TYPE declarations in the file BTREE.DEC here.  }
```

Step 2:   Test your program using the account activity pairs in the file ACCTAMT.DAT.

LABORATORY 11: In-lab Exercise 3

Date .... Section ....

Name ....

When using a B-tree, you may wish to know what percentage of the element fields actually contain elements. This statistic, called the **B-tree element density**, can be computed as follows:

$$\frac{\text{Number of elements}}{\text{Number of nodes} * \text{Maximum number of elements per node}}$$

Step 1: Create a Pascal implementation of the B-tree ADT operation described below.

FUNCTION BTreeDensity (T : BTree) : REAL

Requires:
B-tree T has been created.
Results:
Returns the element density of T. If T is empty, then returns 0.

Step 2: Add your implementation of this operation to the file BTREE.PAS.

Step 3: Add the following code to the test program in the file TEST11.PAS.

```
ELSE IF Cmd = '%'
    THEN WRITELN('Density = ',BTreeDensity(TestTree))
```

Step 4: Prepare a test plan for this operation that covers trees of different shapes and different densities, including a tree of density 1.0 (that is, a tree in which all elements fields contain elements). A test plan form follows.

Step 5: Execute your test plan. If you discover mistakes in your implementation of the BTreeDensity operation, correct them and execute your test plan again.

Test Plan for the BTreeDensity operation			
Test case	*Commands*	*Expected result*	*Checked*

LABORATORY 11: In-lab Exercise 4

Date .... Section ....

Name ....

The **depth** of a node is the length of the path from the root node to the node. The depth of the root node is 1, the root node's children are at depth 2, and so on. This statistic is important because the time it takes to search for a given element is a function of the depth of the node containing the element.

```
FUNCTION BTreeDepth ( T : BTree;
                      SrchKey : BTreeKey ) : INTEGER
```

Requires:
B-tree T has been created.
Results:
If SrchKey is a key in B-tree T, then BTreeDepth returns the depth of the node containing SrchKey. Otherwise, BTreeDepth returns 0.

Step 1: Create a Pascal implementation of this operation.

Step 2: Add your implementation of this operation to the file BTREE.PAS.

 Step 3: Add the following code to the test program in the file TEST11.PAS.

```
ELSE IF ( Cmd = 'D' ) OR ( Cmd = 'd' )
   THEN WRITELN('Depth of 'InputKey,' = ',
                BTreeDepth(Tree,InputKey))
```

You also must change the statement

```
IF ( Cmd = '+' ) OR ( Cmd = '?' )
   THEN READLN(InputKey)
   ELSE READLN;
```

to the statement

```
IF ( Cmd = '+' ) OR ( Cmd = '?' ) OR
   ( Cmd = 'D' ) OR ( Cmd = 'd' )
   THEN READLN(InputKey)
   ELSE READLN;
```

so you can interactively specify the key to be used with the BTreeDepth operation.

Step 4: Prepare a test plan for this operation that covers keys stored at various depths, including test cases in which the key is stored in a root or leaf node, as well as cases in which the key is missing from the tree entirely. A test plan form follows.

Step 5:   Execute your test plan. If you discover mistakes in your implementation of the BTreeDepth operation, correct them and execute your test plan again.

Test Plan for the BTreeDepth operation			
Test case	*Commands*	*Expected result*	*Checked*

LABORATORY 11: Postlab Exercise 1

Date .... Section ....

Name ....

Given a B-tree containing a maximum of M elements per node, what is the minimum number of elements any nonroot node can contain? What is the minimum number of elements the root node can contain? Give examples to illustrate your answer.

LABORATORY 11: Postlab Exercise 2

Date .... Section ....

Name ....

Suppose each node in a B-tree contains a maximum of 64 elements, a relatively large quantity. Briefly describe what change you would make to your implementation of the B-tree ADT to improve performance of the BTreeInsert and BTreeRetrieve operations.

Heap ADT

OVERVIEW

Linked structures are not the only means by which you can represent trees. If you take the binary tree shown below and copy its contents into an array in level order, you produce the following array.

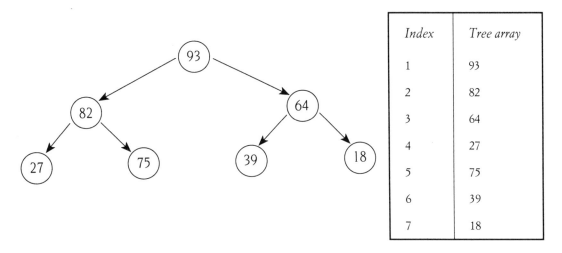

Index	Tree array
1	93
2	82
3	64
4	27
5	75
6	39
7	18

Examining the relationship between positions in the tree and entries in the array, notice that if an element is stored in entry N in the array, then that element's left child is stored in entry 2N, its right child is stored in entry 2N+1, and its parent is stored in entry N MOD 2. These mappings make it possible to move quickly through the tree stepping from parent to child (or vice versa).

Although you could use these mappings to support an array-based implementation of the Binary Search Tree ADT, this laboratory focuses on a different type of tree. A **heap** is a binary tree that meets the following conditions.

- The tree is **complete**. Every level in the tree is full, except possibly the bottom level. If the bottom level is not full, then all missing elements occur on the right.

- Each element in the tree has a corresponding priority value. These priority values determine the relative positions of elements in the tree. For each element E in the tree, all elements in the subtrees below E have priorities that are less than E's priority.

The tree shown above and the tree shown below are both heaps.

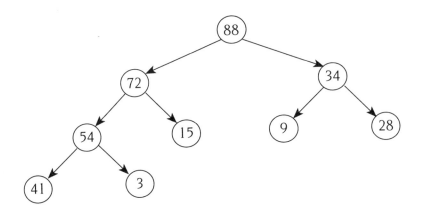

Although the relationship between priorities of the various elements in a heap is not strong enough to support an efficient search for an element with a given priority, this relationship does ensure that the element with the highest priority is at the root of the heap. Furthermore, you can quickly restructure a heap after removing its root element or after inserting a new element. Collectively, these properties describe a data structure that allows you to iterate efficiently through a set of elements based on their priorities (as in the priority queue used in In-lab Exercise 2). In addition, because it is a complete tree, a heap can be constructed within an array without creating gaps in the middle of the array. As a result, a heap can be used as the basis for an efficient sorting algorithm called a **heap sort** (In-lab Exercise 3).

HEAP ADT

ELEMENTS
Each element in a heap has a priority that is used to determine its position in the heap. Elements usually include additional data, as well. Note that the elements in a heap do *not* have unique priorities. In fact, it is quite likely that many elements will have the same priority.

STRUCTURE
The elements form a binary tree. For each element E in the tree, all elements in the subtrees below E have priorities that are less than E's priority.

OPERATIONS

PROCEDURE HeapCreate (VAR H : Heap)

Requires:
None.
Results:
Creates an empty heap H.

```
PROCEDURE HeapInsert ( VAR H : Heap;
                           NewElement : HeapElement )
```

Requires:
Heap H is not full.
Results:
Inserts element NewElement into H. NewElement is initially inserted as the bottom rightmost element in H. It is then moved upward in the heap until the properties that define a heap are restored.

```
PROCEDURE HeapRemoveMax ( VAR H : Heap;
                              VAR MaxElement : HeapElement )
```

Requires:
Heap H is not empty.
Results:
Removes the highest priority element from H and returns it in MaxElement. Replaces the root element with the bottom rightmost element in H. This element is then moved downward in the heap until the properties that define a heap are restored.

```
FUNCTION HeapEmpty ( H : Heap ) : BOOLEAN
```

Requires:
Heap H has been created.
Results:
If H is empty, then returns true. Otherwise, returns false.

```
FUNCTION HeapFull ( H : Heap ) : BOOLEAN
```

Requires:
Heap H has been created.
Results:
If H is full, then returns true. Otherwise, returns false.

```
PROCEDURE HeapClear ( VAR H : Heap )
```

Requires:
Heap H has been created.
Results:
Deletes all elements in H.

```
PROCEDURE HeapShowStructure ( H : Heap )
```

Requires:
Heap H has been created.
Results:
Outputs the elements in heap H in both array and tree forms. If H is empty, then outputs "Empty heap". This operation is intended for debugging purposes only. It assumes that priority values will produce no more than three characters when output.

LABORATORY 12: Cover Sheet

Date .... Section ....

Name ....

Place a check mark in the "Assigned" column next to the exercises your instructor has assigned to your class. Attach this cover sheet to the front of the packet of materials you submit following the laboratory.

	Assigned	*Completed*
Prelab Exercise	✓	
In-lab Exercise 1	✓	
In-lab Exercise 2		
In-lab Exercise 3		
In-lab Exercise 4		
Postlab Exercise 1		
Postlab Exercise 2		
		Total

LABORATORY 12: Prelab Exercise

Date .... Section ....

Name ....

Step 1:   Create a Pascal implementation of the Heap ADT using an array to store the heap elements. Because the heap will change in size, you need to store the index of the bottom rightmost element in the heap (Size) along with the heap elements themselves (Element). Base your implementation on the following TYPE declaration.

```
Heap = RECORD
         Size    : 0..MaxHeapSize;
         Element : ARRAY [1..MaxHeapSize] OF HeapElement;
       END;
```

A CONST declaration defining MaxHeapSize and TYPE declarations of the following form must appear in any program that uses the Heap ADT.

```
HeapPty     = ...
HeapElement = RECORD
                Pty : HeapPty;
                ...
              END;
```

Assume that HeapPty is a type that can be compared using the standard comparison operators ('<', '=', etc.).

An implementation of the HeapShowStructure operation is given in the file SHOW12.PAS.

Step 2:   Create a file called HEAP.DEC that contains the Heap TYPE declaration and a file called HEAP.PAS that contains the routines in your implementation. Include comments that describe the array representation of a heap and the operations in your implementation.

LABORATORY 12: In-lab Exercise 1

Date .... Section ....

Name ....

The test program in the file TEST12.PAS allows you to interactively test your implementation of the Heap ADT using the following commands.

Command	Action
+pty	Insert an element with the specified priority.
–	Remove the element with the highest priority from the heap and output it.
E	Report whether the heap is empty.
F	Report whether the heap is full.
C	Clear the heap.
Q	Quit the test program.

Step 1: Prepare a test plan for your implementation of the Heap ADT. Your test plan should cover heaps of various sizes, including empty, full, and single-element heaps.

Step 2: Execute your test plan. If you discover mistakes in your implementation, correct them and execute your test plan again.

Test Plan for the operations in the Heap ADT			
Test case	*Commands*	*Expected result*	*Checked*

LABORATORY 12: In-lab Exercise 2

Date .... Section ....

Name ....

A **priority queue** is a linear data structure in which elements are maintained in descending order based on priority. Only the highest priority element can be referenced directly, and examining this element entails removing it from the priority queue. A priority queue can be easily and efficiently implemented as a heap, with the HeapInsert operation being used to enqueue elements and the HeapRemoveMax operation being used to dequeue elements.

Operating systems commonly use priority queues to regulate access to a wide variety of system resources including memory, disks, printers, and software utilities. Each time a task requests access to a system resource, the task is placed on the priority queue associated with that resource.

Suppose you wish to model the flow of tasks through a priority queue having the following properties:

- One task is removed from the priority queue every minute (assuming there is at least one task waiting to be removed during that minute).

- From zero to two tasks are added to the priority queue every minute, where there is a 50 chance that no tasks are added, a 25 chance that one task is added, and a 25 chance that two tasks are added.

- Each task added to the priority queue has a priority value in the range 1, 2, . . . ,MaxPtyLevel, where there is an equal chance of the task having any one of these priority values.

By modeling the passage of time using a loop in which every iteration corresponds to one minute of "real" time, you can simulate the flow of tasks through the priority queue using the following approach.

```
Initialize an integer variable Minute to zero.
Create an empty priority queue (heap).
     REPEAT
     If the priority queue (heap) is not empty, then dequeue the task with the highest
        priority (using HeapRemoveMax).
     Compute a random integer value between 0 and 3.
     CASE random value OF
          0,1 : No tasks are added.
          2   : Add one task (using HeapInsert).
          3   : Add two tasks (using HeapInsert).
     END
     Increment Minute.
     UNTIL the specified number of minutes have elapsed.
```

Step 1: Using the program shell given in the file OSSHELL.PAS as a basis, create a Pascal program that uses the Heap ADT to implement the model described above. Your program should update the following information during each simulated minute, that is, during each pass through the loop. (P denotes the priority of the task that was dequeued from the queue during the current minute).

- The total number of tasks of priority P that have been dequeued from the queue.

- The combined length of time that the dequeued tasks of priority P spent waiting in the queue.

- The maximum length of time that any dequeued task of priority P spent waiting in the queue.

In order to compute how long a task has waited in the priority queue, you need to store the "minute" that the task was added to the queue (along with the task's priority) as part of the element corresponding to that task.

Step 2: Use your program to simulate the flow of tasks through a priority queue for 500 minutes and complete the following table.

Number of priority levels (MaxPtyLevel)	Number of tasks dequeued from the queue	Average wait	Longest wait
1	Priority 1:	Priority 1:	Priority 1:
2	Priority 2:	Priority 2:	Priority 2:
	Priority 1:	Priority 1:	Priority 1:
3	Priority 3:	Priority 3:	Priority 3:
	Priority 2:	Priority 2:	Priority 2:
	Priority 1:	Priority 1:	Priority 1:

LABORATORY 12: In-lab Exercise 3

Date .... Section ....

Name ....

You can use a heap to quickly sort an array of elements into ascending order based on priority. Given a list of N unsorted elements, a **heap sort** proceeds as follows.

> Construct a temporary heap from the elements in the list.
> FOR J := N DOWNTO 1 DO
>   Remove the root element from the heap and place it in entry J in the list.

For large lists, it is very costly to use separate arrays to hold the list and the heap. Fortunately, throughout the sorting process, a given element is either in the list or in the heap, but not both. Because the heap occupies a continuous set of array entries beginning with the first entry, you can use the remaining array entries to hold the elements in the list, as shown below.

	Array contents	
Before sorting	Unsorted list elements	
Building the heap	Heap	Unsorted list elements
Heap built	Heap	
Removing from the heap	Heap	Largest list elements (sorted)
After sorting	Sorted list elements	

Step 1: Create a Pascal implementation of the HeapSort procedure described below.

```
PROCEDURE HeapSort ( VAR L : PtyList;
                         N : INTEGER       );
```

Requires:
List L contains an unsorted set of N elements.
Results:
The elements in L are in ascending order based on priority.

An object of type PtyList is an array in which each element has an associated priority. The difference between a PtyList and a heap is that the elements in a PtyList are not in any particular order, while the elements in a heap must conform to the heap conditions described in the Prelab.

   Declare type PtyList to be the same array-based structure you used for type Heap, that is

```
PtyList = Heap;
```

As a result, you can use the same array to store *both* list L and the temporary heap during the HeapSort procedure. Note that all references to the temporary heap should be made using the operations in the Heap ADT.

Step 2:   Create a file called HEAPSORT.PAS containing your HeapSort procedure.

 Step 3:   Before testing your implementation of this procedure using the test program in the file TEST12HS.PAS, prepare a test plan that covers lists of different lengths containing a variety of priority values. Be sure to include lists that have multiple elements with the same priority.

Step 4:   Execute your test plan. If you discover mistakes in your implementation of the HeapSort procedure, correct them and execute your test plan again.

Test Plan for the HeapSort procedure			
Test case	*List*	*Expected result*	*Checked*

LABORATORY 12: In-lab Exercise 4

Date .... Section ....

Name ....

Examining the tree form of a heap rotated ninety degrees counterclockwise from its conventional orientation can be awkward. Because a heap is a complete tree, an unambiguous representation in tree form can be generated by outputting the heap level-by-level, with each level output on a separate line.

PROCEDURE HeapWriteLevels (H : Heap)

Requires:
Heap H has been created.

Results:
Outputs the elements in H in level order, one level per line. Only outputs the priority for each element. If H is empty, then outputs "Empty heap".

Step 1:   Create a Pascal implementation of this operation.

Step 2:   Add your implementation of this operation to the file HEAP.PAS.

Step 3:   Add the following code to the test program in the file TEST12.PAS.

```
ELSE IF ( Cmd = 'W' ) OR ( Cmd = 'w' )
   THEN BEGIN
        WRITELN;
        WRITELN('Levels in tree :');
        HeapWriteLevels(TestHeap);
        WRITELN;
        END
```

Step 4:   Prepare a test plan for the HeapWriteLevels operation that covers heaps of various sizes, including empty and single-element heaps. A test plan form follows.

Step 5:   Execute your test plan. If you discover mistakes in your implementation of the HeapWriteLevels operation, correct them and execute your test plan again.

Test Plan for the HeapWriteLevels operation			
Test case	*Commands*	*Expected result*	*Checked*

LABORATORY 12: Postlab Exercise 1

Date .... Section ....

Name ....

Suppose you have constructed a heap containing two elements with the same priority, E_1 and E_2, as well as other elements with different priorities. If you insert E_1 into the heap before E_2, will your implementation of the Heap ADT always remove E_1 from the heap before it removes E_2? Give examples to illustrate your answer.

LABORATORY 12: Postlab Exercise 2

Date .... Section ....

Name ....

PART A

Given a heap containing ten elements with distinct priorities, where in the heap can the element with the next-to-highest priority be located? Give examples to illustrate your answer.

PART B

Given the same heap as in Part A, where in the heap can the element with the lowest priority be located? Give examples to illustrate your answer.

Weighted Graph ADT

OVERVIEW

Many relationships cannot be expressed easily using either a linear or a hierarchical data structure. The relationship between the cities connected by a highway network is one such relationship. Although it is possible for the roads in a highway network to describe a relationship between cities that is linear (a one-way street, for example) or hierarchical (an expressway and its off-ramps, for instance), we all have driven in circles enough times to know that most highway networks are neither linear nor hierarchical. Thus, we need a data structure that lets us connect each city to any (or all) other cities in the network. This type of data structure is referred to as a **graph**.

Like a tree, a graph consists of a set of nodes (called vertices) and a set of edges. Unlike a tree, an edge in a graph can connect any pair of vertices, not simply a parent and its child. The following graph represents a simple highway network.

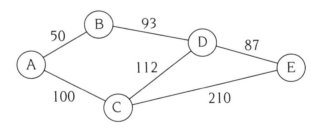

Each vertex in this graph has a unique **label** to denote a particular city. Each edge has a **weight** to denote the cost (measured in terms of distance, time, or money) of traversing the corresponding road. Note that the edges in this graph are **undirected**; that is, if there is an edge connecting a pair of vertices A and B, this edge can be used to move either from A to B or from B to A. The resulting **weighted, undirected graph** expresses the cost of traveling between cities using the highway network. In this laboratory, you focus on the implementation and application of weighted, undirected graphs such as this.

WEIGHTED GRAPH ADT

ELEMENTS
Each vertex in a graph has a label to uniquely identify it. Vertices usually include additional data, as well.

STRUCTURE
The relationship between vertices in a graph is expressed using a set of undirected edges, where each edge connects one pair of vertices. Collectively, these edges define a symmetric relation between vertices. Each edge in a weighted graph has a weight that denotes the cost of traversing that edge.

OPERATIONS

PROCEDURE GraphCreate (VAR G : Graph)

Requires:
None.
Results:
Creates an empty graph G.

PROCEDURE GraphInsertVertex (VAR G : Graph;
                              NewVertex : VertexElement)

Requires:
Graph G is not full.
Results:
Inserts vertex NewVertex into G. If a vertex with the same label as NewVertex already exists in G, then updates that vertex's nonlabel fields with NewVertex's nonlabel fields.

FUNCTION GraphInsertEdge (VAR G : Graph;
                           V1, V2 : VertexLabel;
                           Wt : INTEGER   ) : BOOLEAN

Requires:
Graph G has been created.
Results:
Attempts to insert an edge (with weight Wt) connecting vertices V1 and V2 into G. If both vertices exist in G, then inserts the edge and returns true. If an edge connecting these vertices already exists, replaces the weight of that edge with Wt (and returns true). If either vertex does not exist in G, then returns false.

FUNCTION GraphRetrieveVertex (G : Graph;
                               SrchV : VertexLabel;
                               VAR SrchElement : VertexElement)
                                                 : BOOLEAN

Requires:
Graph G has been created.
Results:
Searches G for vertex SrchV. If this vertex is found, then returns true with SrchElement returning the vertex data. Otherwise, returns false with SrchElement undefined.

```
FUNCTION GraphEdgeWeight ( G : Graph;
                           V1, V2 : VertexLabel;
                           VAR Wt : INTEGER      ) : BOOLEAN
```

Requires:
Graph G has been created.

Results:
Searches G for the edge connecting vertices V1 and V2. If this edge exists, then returns true with Wt returning the weight of this edge. Otherwise, returns false with Wt undefined.

```
FUNCTION GraphEmpty ( G : Graph ) : BOOLEAN
```

Requires:
Graph G has been created.

Results:
If G does not contain any vertices, then returns true. Otherwise, returns false.

```
FUNCTION GraphFull ( G : Graph ) : BOOLEAN
```

Requires:
Graph G has been created.

Results:
If the vertex set for G is full, then returns true. Otherwise, returns false.

```
PROCEDURE GraphClear ( VAR G : Graph )
```

Requires:
Graph G has been created.

Results:
Deletes all vertices and edges in G.

```
PROCEDURE GraphShowStructure ( G : Graph )
```

Requires:
Graph G has been created.

Results:
Outputs G with the vertices in array form and the edges in adjacency matrix form (with edge weights). This operation is intended for debugging purposes only. It assumes that weights will produce no more than four characters when output.

LABORATORY 13: Cover Sheet

Date .... Section ....

Name ....

Place a check mark in the "Assigned" column next to the exercises your instructor has assigned to your class. Attach this cover sheet to the front of the packet of materials you submit following the laboratory.

	Assigned	Completed
Prelab Exercise	✓	
In-lab Exercise 1	✓	
In-lab Exercise 2		
In-lab Exercise 3		
In-lab Exercise 4		
Postlab Exercise 1		
Postlab Exercise 2		
		Total

LABORATORY 13: Prelab Exercise

Date .... Section ....

Name ....

You can represent a graph in several ways. In this laboratory, you use an array to store the set of vertices and an **adjacency matrix** to store the set of edges. An entry [J,K] in an adjacency matrix contains information on the edge that goes from the vertex with index J to the vertex with index K. For a weighted graph, each matrix entry indicates whether the corresponding edge is included in the graph and, if it is included, the weight of the edge.

The following vertex array and adjacency matrix represent the weighted graph shown on the first page of this laboratory. A "—" is used to denote an edge missing from the graph.

Vertex array	
Index	*Label*
1	A
2	B
3	C
4	D
5	E

Adjacency matrix					
From\To	*1*	*2*	*3*	*4*	*5*
1	—	50	100	—	—
2	50	—	—	93	—
3	100	—	—	112	210
4	—	93	112	—	87
5	—	—	210	87	—

Step 1: Create a Pascal implementation of the Weighted Graph ADT using an array to store the vertex elements (Vertex) and an adjacency matrix to store the edges (Edge). Each entry in the vertex array should have a unique label (Vertex[ ].VLabel). Each entry in the adjacency matrix should indicate whether the corresponding edge is included in the graph (Edge[,].Exists) and, if it is included, the edge's weight (Edge[,].Weight). Because the number of vertices in a graph is not fixed, you also need to keep track of how many vertices are in the graph (Size). Base your implementation on the following TYPE declarations.

```
VertexArray = ARRAY [ 1..MaxGraphSize ] OF VertexElement;

EdgeElement = RECORD
                  Exists : BOOLEAN;
                  Weight : INTEGER;
              END;
```

```
AdjMatrix   = ARRAY [ 1..MaxGraphSize,
                      1..MaxGraphSize  ] OF EdgeElement;

Graph       = RECORD
                 Size   : 0..MaxGraphSize;
                 Vertex : VertexArray;
                 Edge   : AdjMatrix;
              END;
```

A CONST declaration defining MaxGraphSize and TYPE declarations of the following form must appear in any program that uses the Weighted Graph ADT.

```
VertexLabel   = ...
VertexElement = RECORD
                   VLabel : VertexLabel;
                   ...
                END;
```

Assume that VertexLabel is a type that can be compared using the standard comparison operators ('<', '=', etc.).

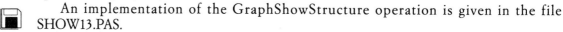

An implementation of the GraphShowStructure operation is given in the file SHOW13.PAS.

Step 2: Create a file called WTGRAPH.DEC containing the VertexArray, EdgeElement, AdjMatrix, and Graph TYPE declarations and a file called WTGRAPH.PAS containing the routines in your implementation. Include comments that describe the representation of a weighted graph and the operations in your implementation.

LABORATORY 13: In-lab Exercise 1

Date .... Section ....

Name ....

The test program in the file TEST13.PAS allows you to interactively test your implementation of the Weighted Graph ADT using the following commands.

Command	Action
+V	Insert vertex V.
=VW Wt	Insert an edge (with weight Wt) connecting vertices V and W.
?V	Retrieve vertex V and output it.
#VW	Retrieve the edge connecting vertices V and W and output its weight.
E	Report whether the graph is empty.
F	Report whether the graph is full.
C	Clear the graph.
Q	Quit the test program.

Step 1: Prepare a test plan for your implementation of the Weighted Graph ADT. Your test plan should cover graphs in which vertices are connected in a variety of ways. Be sure to include test cases that attempt to retrieve edges that do not exist or that connect nonexistent vertices. A test plan form follows.

Step 2: Execute your test plan. If you discover mistakes in your implementation, correct them and execute your test plan again.

Test Plan for the operations in the Weighted Graph ADT			
Test case	*Commands*	*Expected result*	*Checked*

LABORATORY 13: In-lab Exercise 2

Date .... Section ....

Name ....

In many applications of weighted graphs, you need to determine not only whether there is an edge connecting a pair of vertices, but whether there is a path connecting them. By extending the concept of an adjacency matrix, you can produce a **path matrix** in which an entry [J,K] contains information on the shortest path from the vertex with index J to the vertex with index K. The following path matrix is derived from the graph shown on the first page of this laboratory.

Vertex array			Path matrix					
Index	*Label*		*From\To*	*1*	*2*	*3*	*4*	*5*
1	A		1	0	50	100	143	230
2	B		2	50	0	150	93	180
3	C		3	100	150	0	112	199
4	D		4	143	93	112	0	87
5	E		5	230	180	199	87	0

Suppose you wish to know the cost of the shortest path from vertex A to vertex E. The cost of this path, 230, is stored in entry [1,5] in the path matrix (the corresponding path is ABDE). In creating this path matrix, we have assumed that a path of cost 0 exists from a vertex to itself (entries of the form [J,J]). This assumption is based on the view that traveling from a vertex to itself is a nonevent and thus costs nothing. Depending on how you intend to apply the information in a graph, you may want to use a different assumption.

Given the adjacency matrix for a graph, we begin construction of the path matrix by noting that all edges are paths. These one-edge-long paths are combined to form two-edge-long paths by applying the following reasoning.

> IF there exists a path from a vertex J to a vertex M and
> there exists a path from a vertex M to a vertex K
> THEN there exists a path from vertex J to vertex K.

We can apply this same reasoning to these newly generated paths to form paths consisting of more and more edges. The key to this process is to enumerate and combine paths in a complete and efficient manner. One approach is described in the following algorithm.

- Initialize the path matrix so that it is the same as the edge matrix (all edges are paths). In addition, create a path from each of cost 0 vertex to itself.

- FOR M := 1 TO number of vertices DO
    FOR J := 1 TO number of vertices DO
        FOR K := 1 TO number of vertices DO
            IF there exists a path from vertex J to vertex M and
            there exists a path from vertex M to vertex K
            THEN Add a path from vertex J to vertex K to the path matrix.

Note that variables J, K, and M refer to vertex indices, *not* vertex labels. This algorithm establishes the existence of paths between vertices, but not their costs. Fortunately, by extending the reasoning used above, we can easily determine the cost of the shortest path between vertices.

IF there exists a path from a vertex J to a vertex M and
    there exists a path from a vertex M to a vertex K and
    either we have not yet found a path from vertex J to vertex K or
        the cost of the existing path is more than the sum of the costs of the
        paths from J to M and from M to K
    THEN the path JMK is the shortest path from vertex J to vertex K that we
        have found so far.

Incorporating this reasoning into the previous algorithm yields the following algorithm.

- Initialize the path matrix so it is the same as the edge matrix (all edges are paths). In addition, create a path of cost 0 from each vertex to itself.

- FOR M := 1 TO number of vertices DO
    FOR J := 1 TO number of vertices DO
        FOR K := 1 TO number of vertices DO
            IF there exists a path from vertex J to vertex M and
                there exists a path from vertex M to vertex K and
                either there is *not* a path from vertex J to vertex K or
                    the cost of the existing path from J to K is higher than
                    the sum of the costs of the paths from J to M and
                    from M to K
            THEN Add a path from vertex J to vertex K to the path matrix.
                The cost of the path is the sum of the costs of the paths
                from J to M and from M to K.

Once again, variables J, K, and M refer to vertex indices, *not* vertex labels.

Step 1:   Create a Pascal implementation of the GraphComputePaths operation described below.

```
PROCEDURE GraphComputePaths ( VAR G : Graph )
```

Requires:

Graph G has been created.

Results:

Computes the path matrix for graph G.

Your implementation should represent the path matrix using a matrix of type AdjMatrix. Each entry in the path matrix (Path) should indicate whether there is a path between the corresponding pair of vertices (Path[,].Exists) and, if such paths exist, the cost of the shortest path (Path[,].Weight). Base your implementation on the following TYPE declaration.

```
Graph = RECORD
          Size   : 0..MaxGraphSize;
          Vertex : VertexArray;
          Edge,
          Path   : AdjMatrix;
        END;
```

Step 2: Modify the declaration of type Graph in the file WTGRAPH.DEC to include the Path matrix.

Step 3: Add your implementation of the GraphComputePaths operation to the routines in the file WTGRAPH.PAS.

Step 4: Add the following code to the GraphShowStructure routine in the file SHOW13.PAS.

```
WRITELN('Path matrix');
PrintMatrix(G.Path,G.Size);
```

Step 5: Add the following call immediately after the REPEAT statement in the test program in the file TEST13.PAS.

```
GraphComputePaths(TestGraph);
```

Step 6: Prepare a test plan for the GraphComputePaths operation that includes graphs in which vertices are connected in a variety of ways with a variety of weights. Be sure to include test cases in which an edge connecting a pair of vertices has a higher cost than a multiedge path between these same vertices. The edge CE and the path CDE in the graph shown on the first page of this laboratory have this property. A test plan form follows.

Step 7: Execute your test plan. If you discover mistakes in your implementation of the GraphComputePaths operation, correct them and execute your test plan again.

Test Plan for the GraphComputePaths operation			
Test case	*Commands*	*Expected result*	*Checked*

LABORATORY 13: In-lab Exercise 3

Date .... Section ....

Name ....

Suppose you wish to create a road map of a particular highway network. In order to avoid causing confusion among map users, you must be careful to color the cities in such a way that no cities sharing a common border also share the same color. An assignment of colors to cities that meets this criterion is called a **proper coloring** of the map.

Restating this problem in terms of a graph, an assignment of colors to the vertices in a graph is a proper coloring of the graph if no vertex is assigned the same color as an adjacent vertex. The assignment of colors (grey and white) in the following graph is an example of a proper coloring.

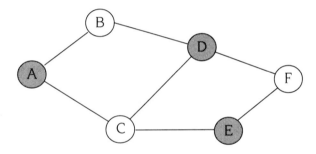

Two colors are not always enough to produce a proper coloring. One of the most famous theorems in graph theory, the Four-Color Theorem, states that creating a proper coloring of any **planar graph** (that is, any graph that can be drawn on a sheet of paper without having the edges cross one another) requires using at most four colors. A planar graph that requires four colors is shown below. (Note that if a graph is not planar, you may need to use more than four colors.)

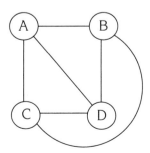

Step 1:   Create a Pascal implementation of the following operation.

```
FUNCTION GraphProperColoring ( G : Graph ) : BOOLEAN
```

Requires:
Each vertex in graph G has been assigned a color.
Results:
If no vertex in G has the same color as an adjacent vertex, then returns true. Otherwise, returns false.

Assume that colors are represented as characters ('R' for red, and so on) and that each vertex has a field that stores the color of the vertex (Vertex[ ].Color). Base your implementation on the following TYPE declaration.

```
VertexElement = RECORD
                    VLabel :  VertexLabel;
                    Color  :  CHAR;
                    ...
                END;
```

Step 2:   Add your implementation of the GraphProperColoring operation to the routines in the file WTGRAPH.PAS.

Step 3:   Replace the loop that outputs the vertex array in the GraphShowStructure procedure in the file SHOW13.PAS with the following loop.

```
WRITELN('Vertices:');
FOR J := 1 TO G.Size DO
    WRITELN(J:2,' ',G.Vertex[J].VLabel,
              ' ',G.Vertex[J].Color  );
```

Step 4:   The test program in the file TEST13CL.PAS lets you test your implementation of the GraphProperColoring operation using the following commands.

Command	Action
+VC	Insert vertex V with color C.
=VW	Insert an edge connecting vertices V and W. This edge is assigned a weight of 1.
C	Clear the graph.
Q	Quit the test program.

Step 5:   Prepare a test plan for this operation that includes a variety of graphs and vertex color assignments. A test plan form follows.

Step 6:   Execute your test plan. If you discover mistakes in your implementation of the GraphProperColoring operation, correct them and execute your test plan again.

Test Plan for the GraphProperColoring operation			
Test case	*Commands*	*Expected result*	*Checked*

Test Plan for the expression parsing program			
Test case	*Expression*	*Expected result*	*Checked*

LABORATORY 14: In-lab Exercise 3

Date .... Section ....

Name ....

Deleting elements from a hash table is not quite as simple as inserting or retrieving them. Simply marking deleted hash table entries as empty eventually blocks the retrieval process for other keys. For example, if you were to delete the element with key 184 from the following table by marking table entry 4 as empty (Hash(184)=4),

Index	Key
0	70
1	89
2	—
3	23
4	184
5	33
6	—
7	37
8	—
9	9

then subsequent searches for the element with key 33 using linear probing would incorrectly fail at entry 4 (Hash(33)=3).

Instead of marking the deleted element as empty, you need to designate the element as having been deleted using another special key value, HTableDelKey. Use a value of –2 for HTableDelKey. You also need to modify your implementation of the Hash Table ADT so it treats entries with this key value as either empty (HTableInsert) or full (HTableRetrieve), depending on the operation.

Step 1: Create a Pascal implementation of the following operation.

```
FUNCTION HTableDelete ( VAR H : HTable;
                          DelKey : HTableKey ) : BOOLEAN
```

Requires:
Hash table H has been created.
Results:
Deletes the element with key DelKey from H. Returns true if this element exists (and is deleted). Otherwise, returns false.

Step 2: Create a file called HASHDEL.DEC that contains the TYPE declaration in the file HASHLNR.DEC and a file called HASHDEL.PAS that contains your implementation of the HTableDelete operation along with modified versions of the remaining operations in the Hash Table ADT.

 Step 3: Add the following code to the test program in the file TEST14.PAS.

```
ELSE IF Cmd = '-'
   THEN BEGIN
        IF HTableDelete(TestTable,InputKey)
           THEN WRITELN('Deleted')
           ELSE WRITELN('Not found');
        END
```

You also must change the statement

```
IF ( Cmd = '+' ) OR ( Cmd = '?' )
   THEN READLN(InputKey)
   ELSE READLN;
```

to the statement

```
IF ( Cmd = '+' ) OR ( Cmd = '?' ) OR ( Cmd = '-' )
   THEN READLN(InputKey)
   ELSE READLN;
```

so you can interactively specify the key value to be used with the HTableDelete operation.

Step 4: Add the following CONST declaration to the test program

```
HTableDelKey = -2
```

to declare the special key value for the deleted element marker.

Step 5: Modify the test program so the declarations and routines that support deletion (HASHDEL.DEC and HASHDEL.PAS) are included in place of the ones you created in the Prelab.

Step 6: Prepare a test plan for your modified implementation of the Hash Table ADT that includes tables containing a variety of keys. Be sure to include test cases that require linear probing across deleted entries. A test plan form follows.

Step 7: Execute your test plan. If you discover mistakes in your implementation, correct them and execute your test plan again.

Test Plan for the operations in the Hash Table ADT (including deletion)			
Test case	*Commands*	*Expected result*	*Checked*

LABORATORY 14: In-lab Exercise 4

Date .... Section ....

Name ....

One disadvantage of linear probing is that a set of keys that hash to the same table entry will remain grouped together near that entry, a phenomenon known as **clustering**. This problem is only made worse by linear probing's tendency to interleave clusters to form still larger clusters. To reduce clustering, you need a better mechanism for resolving collisions—one that distributes elements that collide throughout the table, rather than leaving them clustered together. Many such mechanisms exist. In this exercise, you examine one of these, a collision resolution mechanism called **double hashing**.

Suppose a key hashes to table entry I; that is, I=Hash(Key). Linear probing will explore the sequence of hash table entries with array indices

```
( I + 1 ) MOD N
( I + 2 ) MOD N
( I + 3 ) MOD N
. . .
```

until the appropriate table entry is found. In double hashing, this sequence is replaced by the sequence

```
( I + S )   MOD N
( I + 2*S ) MOD N
( I + 3*S ) MOD N
. . .
```

where the **step size** S is produced using a different hash function than was used to produce I.

$$S = StepSize(Key) = Key \; MOD \; (N - 2) + 1$$

The advantage of double hashing is that two keys that hash to the same table entry are unlikely to also produce the same step size, so it is unlikely that these keys will form a cluster. For example, if you use the remainder hash function in conjunction with a hash table of size 19, then all keys in the table below will hash to entry 5. The step size for each key is different, however, leading to different probe sequences when double hashing is used to resolve collisions.

Key	I	S	Sequence of entries probed
5	5	6	5,11,17,4,10,16,...
24	5	8	5,13,2,10,18,7,...
81	5	14	5,0,14,9,4,18,...
119	5	1	5,6,7,8,9,10,...
157	5	5	5,10,15,1,6,11,...

Step 1: Modify your implementation of the Hash Table ADT so it uses double hashing instead of linear probing.

Step 2: Create a file called HASHDBL.DEC that contains the TYPE declaration in the file HASHLNR.DEC and a file called HASHDBL.PAS that contains the routines in your modified implementation of the Hash Table ADT.

Step 3: Modify the test program in the file TEST14.PAS so that the declarations and routines that support double hashing (HASHDBL.DEC and HASHDBL.PAS) are included in place of the ones you created in the prelab.

Step 4: Prepare a test plan for your implementation that covers a variety of hash tables. Be sure to include test cases in which many keys hash to the same table entry.

Step 5: Execute your test plan. If you discover mistakes in your implementation, correct them and execute your test plan again.

Test Plan for the operations in the Hash Table ADT (including double hashing)			
Test case	*Commands*	*Expected result*	*Checked*

LABORATORY 14: Postlab Exercise 1

Date .... Section ....

Name ....

Given a set of N distinct keys, develop worst-case, order-of-magnitude estimates of the execution time of following Hash Table ADT operations, assuming they are implemented using a remainder hash function in conjunction with linear probing. Briefly explain your reasoning behind each estimate.

	HTableInsert	O( )

Explanation:

	HTableRetrieve	O( )

Explanation:

LABORATORY 14: Postlab Exercise 2

Date .... Section ....

Name ....

When using double hashing to resolve collisions (In-lab Exercise 4), we can be sure that we can fill the entire hash table if both the table size (N) and the divisor used in producing the step size (N-2) are prime numbers. Consider the case in which the size of the hash table is 6. What problem can be caused by the combination of the remainder hash function

$$Hash(Key) = Key \; MOD \; 6$$

and the step size hash function

$$StepSize(Key) = Key \; MOD \; 4 + 1$$

when double hashing is used to resolve collisions?

Performance Evaluation

OVERVIEW

In other laboratories, you analyze a variety of routines and develop worst-case, order-of-magnitude estimates of their execution times. Generally, you express these estimates as a function of the number of data items (N) a routine manipulates in performing its task. The results are estimates of the form O(N), O(LogN), and so forth.

Although these estimates allow you to group routines based on their worst-case performance, they are by their very nature abstract estimates. They do not take into account factors specific to a particular environment, such as how a routine is implemented, the type of computer system on which it is being run, and the kind of data being input. If you are to determine accurately how well or poorly a given routine will perform in a given environment, you need to evaluate the routine in that environment.

In this laboratory, you measure the performance of a variety of routines. You begin by developing a set of tools that allow you to measure execution time. Then you use these tools to measure the execution times of these routines as they process several different data sets.

You can determine a routine's execution time in a number of ways. The timings performed in this laboratory will be generated using the approach summarized below.

> Get the current system time (call this InitTime).
> Execute the routine.
> Get the current system time (call this FinalTime).
> The routine's execution time = FinalTime − InitTime.

If the routine executes rapidly, then the difference between InitTime and FinalTime may be too small for your computer system to measure. In this case, you will need to execute the routine several times and divide the resulting time interval by the number of repetitions, as follows:

> Get the current system time (call this InitTime).
> Execute the routine M times.
> Get the current system time (call this FinalTime).
> The routine's execution time = (FinalTime − InitTime) / M.

To use this approach, you must have some method for getting and storing the "current system time." How the current system time is defined and accessed varies from system to system. We have outlined two common methods below.

METHOD 1

Use a procedure/function call to get the current time of day. Store this information in a variable of the following type.

```
SystemTime = RECORD
            Hour,          {  Hour    0-23           }
            Minute,        {  Minute 0-59            }
            Second,        {  Second 0-59            }
            Fraction       {  Fraction of a second   }
                 : INTEGER;
            END;
```

The range of values for the Fraction field depends on the resolution of the system clock. Common ranges are 0–99 (hundredths of a second) and 0–999 (thousandths of a second). This method is effective on systems where the routine being timed is the only program running.

METHOD 2

Use a procedure/function call to get the amount of processor time (in thousandths or ten thousandths of a second) that *you* have used since logging on. Store this information in a variable of the following type.

```
SystemTime = INTEGER;
```

This method should be used on multiuser or multiprocess systems where the routine being timed is *not* the only program running.

LABORATORY 15: Cover Sheet

Date .... Section ....

Name ....

Place a check mark in the "Assigned" column next to the exercises your instructor has assigned to your class. Attach this cover sheet to the front of the packet of materials you submit following the laboratory.

	Assigned	*Completed*
Prelab Exercise	✓	
In-lab Exercise 1	✓	
In-lab Exercise 2		
In-lab Exercise 3		
In-lab Exercise 4		
Postlab Exercise 1		
Postlab Exercise 2		
		Total

LABORATORY 15: Prelab Exercise

Date .... Section ....

Name ....

Step 1: Select one of the methods for determining the current system time described above (along with the corresponding TYPE declaration), and create Pascal implementations of the following routines.

```
PROCEDURE CurrentTime ( VAR T : SystemTime )
```

Inputs:
None.
Outputs:
T returns the current system time.

```
FUNCTION ElapsedTime ( InitTime,
                       FinalTime : SystemTime ) : INTEGER
```

Inputs:
InitTime and FinalTime contain valid system times, and FinalTime follows InitTime.
Outputs:
Returns the difference between InitTime and FinalTime.

Be careful not to exceed the limits of variables of type INTEGER when computing the elapsed time.

Step 2: Create a file called TIME.DEC that contains the appropriate SystemTime TYPE declaration and a file called TIME.PAS that contains your CurrentTime procedure and ElapsedTime function.

Step 3: What is the resolution of your CurrentTime procedure (in fractions of a second)?

Step 4: What length time intervals can your ElapsedTime function handle without exceeding the limits of type INTEGER?

LABORATORY 15: In-lab Exercise 1

Date .... Section ....

Name ....

Step 1: Prepare a test plan for your CurrentTime procedure.

Step 2: Execute your test plan. If you discover mistakes in your CurrentTime procedure, correct them and execute your test plan again.

Test Plan for the CurrentTime procedure			
Test case	*Current system time*	*Expected result*	*Checked*

Step 3: Prepare a test plan for your ElapsedTime function. Be sure to include test cases in which minute, hour, and day transitions occur between InitTime and FinalTime.

Step 4: Execute your test plan. If you discover mistakes in your ElapsedTime function, correct them and execute your test plan again.

Test Plan for the ElapsedTime function			
Test case	*InitTime and FinalTime*	*Expected result*	*Checked*

LABORATORY 15: In-lab Exercise 2

Date .... Section ....

Name ....

 In this exercise, you examine the performance of the searching routines given in the file SEARCH.PAS.

 Step 1:   Use the program in the file TIMESRCH.PAS to measure the execution times of the LinearSearch and BinarySearch routines. This program begins by generating an ordered list of integer keys (KeyList) and a set of keys to search for in this list (SearchSet). It then measures the amount of time it takes to search for these keys using the specified routine and computes the average time per search.

Three different test classes are supported by this program, where NumKeys is a user-supplied input that specifies the number of keys in KeyList.

All searches succeed

- KeyList contains 2,4,...,(2*NumKeys).

- SearchSet contains keys that are in KeyList, and are equally spaced throughout the list.

No searches succeed

- KeyList contains 2,4,...,(2*NumKeys).

- SearchSet contains keys that are *not* in KeyList, but are equally spaced throughout the range of values in the list.

Randomly generated

- KeyList and SearchSet contain randomly generated keys in the range from 1 through 2*NumKeys.

Step 2:   Complete the following table by measuring the execution times of the LinearSearch and BinarySearch routines for each combination of these three test classes and the three values of NumKeys listed in the table.

Note that your instructor may want you to use values of NumKeys that differ from those listed in this table. Confirm that these values are accurate before continuing.

Routine	Number of keys in list (NumKeys)		
	1000	2000	4000
LinearSearch O(N)			
All searches succeed			
No searches succeed			
Randomly generated			
BinarySearch O(LogN)			
All searches succeed			
No searches succeed			
Randomly generated			

Times shown are in _____ of a second

Step 3: How well do your measured times conform with the worst-case, order-of-magnitude estimates given for these routines?

Step 4: Use the program in the file TIMESRCH.PAS to measure the execution times of the Unknown1Search and Unknown2Search routines and complete the table below.

Note that your instructor may want you to use values of NumKeys that differ from those listed in this table. Confirm that these values are accurate before continuing.

	Number of keys in list (NumKeys)		
Routine	*1000*	*2000*	*4000*
Unknown1Search O( )			
All searches succeed			
No searches succeed			
Randomly generated			
Unknown2Search O( )			
All searches succeed			
No searches succeed			
Randomly generated			

Times shown are in _____ of a second

Step 5: Using your measured times as a basis, develop order-of-magnitude estimates of the execution times of the Unknown1Search and Unknown2Search routines. Briefly explain your reasoning behind each estimate.

LABORATORY 15: In-lab Exercise 3

Date .... Section ....

Name ....

In this exercise, you examine the performance of the set of sorting routines given in the file SORT.PAS.

Step 1: Use the program in the file TIMESORT.PAS to measure the execution times of the SelectionSort and QuickSort routines. This program begins by generating a list of integer keys (KeyList). It then measures the amount of time it takes to sort this list into ascending order using the specified routine.

Three different test classes are supported by this program, where NumKeys is a user-supplied input that specifies the number of keys in KeyList.

Ascending order

- KeyList contains 1,2,...,NumKeys.

Descending order

- KeyList contains NumKeys,NumKeys–1,...,1.

Randomly generated

- KeyList contains randomly generated keys in the range from 1 through 2*NumKeys.

Step 2: Complete the following table by measuring the execution times of the SelectionSort and QuickSort routines for each combination of these three test classes and the three values of NumKeys listed in the table.

Note that your instructor may want you to use values of NumKeys that differ from those listed in this table. Confirm that these values are accurate before continuing.

| | Number of keys in list (NumKeys) | | |
Routine	1000	2000	4000
SelectionSort O(N²)			
Ascending order			
Descending order			
Randomly generated			
QuickSort O(NLogN)			
Ascending order			
Descending order			
Randomly generated			

Times shown are in _____ of a second

Step 3: How well do your measured times conform with the worst-case, order-of-magnitude estimates given for these routines?

Step 4: Use the program in the file TIMESORT.PAS to measure the execution times of the Unknown1Sort and Unknown2Sort routines and complete the table below.

Note that your instructor may want you to use values of NumKeys that differ from those listed in this table. Confirm that these values are accurate before continuing.

	Number of keys in list (NumKeys)		
Routine	*1000*	*2000*	*4000*
Unknown1Sort O( )			
Ascending order			
Descending order			
Randomly generated			
Unknown2Sort O( )			
Ascending order			
Descending order			
Randomly generated			

Times shown are in _____ of a second

Step 5:   Using your measured times as a basis, develop order-of-magnitude estimates of the execution times of the Unknown1Sort and Unknown2Sort routines. Briefly explain your reasoning behind each estimate.

LABORATORY 15: In-lab Exercise 4

Date .... Section ....

Name ....

In this exercise, you measure the performance of the Stack ADT implementations you created in Laboratory 4.

Step 1: Using the tools you created in the Prelab as a basis, construct a Pascal program that measures the execution times of the Push and Pop operations in a given implementation of the Stack ADT. Because these operations execute so rapidly, you need to call each operation a number of times and then compute the average time taken by a call to that operation.

Step 2: Use your program to measure the execution times of your array and linked list implementations of the Push and Pop operations, and complete the table below.

If your compiler allows you to enable/disable **run-time error-checking** (that is, range-checks, overflow-checks, and so on), then for each implementation

- measure the execution times of the Push and Pop operations with run-time error-checking **enabled.**

- *recompile your implementation* and repeat these measurements with run-time error-checking **disabled**.

If your compiler does *not* permit you to enable/disable run-time error-checking, then perform these measurements using the default error-checking mode.

	Execution time	
Stack ADT	*Error-checking enabled*	*Error-checking disabled*
Array implementation		
Push		
Pop		
Linked list implementation		
Push		
Pop		

Times shown are in _____ of a second

Date .... Section ....

Name ....

You are given a pair of searching routines. Both routines have worst-case, order-of-magnitude execution time estimates of O(N). When you measure the actual execution times of these routines on a given system using a variety of different data sets, you discover that one routine consistently executes five times faster than the other. How can both routines be O(N), yet have different execution times when they are compared using the same system and the same data?

LABORATORY 15: Postlab Exercise 2

Date .... Section ....

Name ....

Using your measurements from In-lab Exercises 2 and 3 as a basis, estimate the execution times of the routines listed below for a randomly generated list of 8,000 integer keys. Do *not* measure the actual execution times of these routines using a list of this size. Estimate what you think their execution times will be based on the measurements you have already done. Briefly explain your reasoning behind each estimate.

Routine	*Number of keys in list (NumKeys)* 8,000
Linear Search	Estimated execution time:
Explanation:	
Binary Search	Estimated execution time:
Explanation:	

Times shown are in _____ of a second

Routine	*Number of keys in list (NumKeys)* *8,000*
SelectionSort	Estimated execution time:
Explanation:	
QuickSort	Estimated execution time:
Explanation:	

Times shown are in _____ of a second